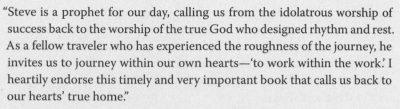

"Steve is a prophet for our day, calling us from the idolatrous worship of success back to the worship of the true God who designed rhythm and rest. As a fellow traveler who has experienced the roughness of the journey, he invites us to journey within our own hearts—'to work within the work.' I heartily endorse this timely and very important book that calls us back to our hearts' true home."

Nelson Okanya, president, Eastern Mennonite Missions

"In most of my leadership training, including as a Harvard MBA, the focus was largely outward—on assessments, strategies, results, etc.—with very little focus on me, my character and my spiritual formation. I've learned through the years, however, and often the hard way, that my leadership effectiveness in both Christian ministry and the commercial marketplace has much more to do with my character than my ideas. *Inside Job* shows us the way to lead more effectively from the inside out."

Tripp Johnston, executive director, SIM's Sports Friends Ministry

"We run as hard as we can in the pursuit of success and contentment only to find out that true success, contentment and transformation come from the 'inside job.' I highly recommend this book as a place for you to begin your inside work."

Mark Linsz, former treasurer of Bank of America, cofounder and senior managing partner of My Next Season

"*Inside Job* provokes honest reflection and heartfelt response that invites the reader into a deeper walk with Christ—a journey of steadfast resilience toward a life of love. Quite countercultural in his approach, Steve Smith encourages the reader to consider traveling the descent of Christlike humility rather than the ascent of worldly success."

Stephen Macchia, Leadership Transformations, Inc., author of *Crafting a Rule of Life*

"Nothing of eternal significance can flow out of a hollow life. As spiritual leaders, we can only minister out of the abundance of our heart and soul. Thus, each of us must do our own interior work to do God's work in a God-honoring way. Stephen Smith's *Inside Job* shows us how."

Wil Hernandez, executive director of CenterQuest

"Like a laser beam, *Inside Job* penetrates to the heart of what Christian leadership is all about. In a day and age when much of leadership centers around an array of tips and techniques, Steve Smith takes us to the true focus of leadership—character. . . . His wisdom, insights and straight-forward approach will lead you to understand that leadership success is truly an inside-out job. . . . This is a must read for those who truly want to lead in the way of Christ!"

Randy Rains, associate vice president, International Mission Board, SBC

"It is a sobering reality that many of us as leaders plunge ahead in the work we do, the relationships that we develop and the lifestyle that we adopt without a realistic perspective of what drives us. This subverts what ought to be joy, and makes us susceptible to failure or burnout. Stephen Smith offers us in *Inside Job* a path for proper self-examination. . . . Read this book with an open mind and heart and you will know God and yourself much better. The people around you will be glad for it."

Mel Lawrenz, minister at large, Elmbrook Church

"After years of working in the public eye as an executive, I found life-giving wisdom and much needed solutions among the private pages of *Inside Job*. With the firmness of a loving father and the frankness of a caring mentor, author Stephen W. Smith writes with deep understanding of a leader's journey, offering practical applications you can apply with the turn of nearly every page."

Dusty Rhodes, WAY Media, Inc., senior vice president

"Leadership is an exceptionally complex role, and the leader's primary re-sponsibility is toward those whom they influence. Steve offers not only helpful leadership guidance but, even more importantly, a crucial call to deeper waters of formation in Christ. Steve's work provides needed di-rection amidst the demands of today's leadership so that leaders may in-fluence others well. Don't just read this book, pray and live it."

Scott E. Shaum, director of staff development, Barnabas International

"As a personal trainer for our soul, Steve first helps us confront with brutal honesty the vulnerability of our souls and the wounds of our hearts. . . . Read this slowly and let it begin an 'inside job' in the deep and hidden parts of your life. You will find that you will become who you long to be, to the benefit of your own soul and everyone around you!"

Scott Arbeiter, former lead pastor at Elmbrook Church

INSIDE JOB

DOING THE
WORK WITHIN
THE WORK

Stephen W. Smith

IVP Books

An imprint of InterVarsity Press
Downers Grove, Illinois

InterVarsity Press
P.O. Box 1400, Downers Grove, IL 60515-1426
ivpress.com
email@ivpress.com
©2015 by Stephen W. Smith

InterVarsity Press® is the book-publishing division of InterVarsity Christian Fellowship/USA®, a movement of students and faculty active on campus at hundreds of universities, colleges and schools of nursing in the United States of America, and a member movement of the International Fellowship of Evangelical Students. For information about local and regional activities, visit intervarsity.org.

Scripture quotations, unless otherwise noted, are from The Message. Copyright © 1993, 1994, 1995. Used by permission of NavPress Publishing Group. All rights reserved.

While any stories in this book are true, some names and identifying information may have been changed to protect the privacy of individuals.

"Patient Trust" by Pierre Teilhard de Chardin from Hearts on Fire: Praying with Jesuits (Chicago: Loyola Press, 2005). Used by permission:

Cover design: Cindy Kiple
Interior design: Beth McGill
Images: © ToddSm66/iStockphoto

ISBN 978-0-8308-4428-9 (print)
ISBN 978-0-8308-6487-4 (digital)

Printed in the United States of America ∞

Library of Congress Cataloging-in-Publication Data

Smith, Stephen W., 1954-
  Inside job : doing the work within the work / Stephen W. Smith.
      pages cm
  Includes bibliographical references.
  ISBN 978-0-8308-4428-9 (pbk. : alk. paper)
  1. Leadership—Religious aspects—Christianity. 2. Character. 3. Spiritual life—Christianity. 4. Fruit of the Spirit. I. Title.
  BV4597.53.L43S65 2015
  248.8'9—dc23

                                                                    2015013534

| P | 20 | 19 | 18 | 17 | 16 | 15 | 14 | 13 | 12 | 11 | 10 | 9 | 8 | 7 | 6 | 5 | 4 | 3 | 2 | 1 |
| Y | 31 | 30 | 29 | 28 | 27 | 26 | 25 | 24 | 23 | 22 | 21 | 20 | 19 | 18 | 17 | 16 | 15 |

So that we would never forget!

CONTENTS

Part One

THE CRISIS IN THE LEADER'S SOUL

◆

LONG AGO A CHINESE MAN began his career making bell stands for the huge bronze bells that hung in Buddhist temples. This man became prized and celebrated for making the best, most elaborate and enduring bell stands in the entire region. No other person could make the bell stands with such strength and beauty. His reputation grew vast and his skill was in high demand. One day the celebrated woodcarver was asked, "Please tell us the secret of your success!" He replied:

> Long before I start making and carving the bell stand, I go into the forest to do the work before the work. I look at all of the hundreds of trees to find the ideal tree—already formed by God to become a bell stand. I look for the boughs of the tree to be massive, strong and already shaped. It takes a long time to find the right tree. But without doing the work before the work, I could not do what I have accomplished.

1

Life Is More Than Chasing Success

◆

The ground at the foot of the ladder of success is littered with the names, faces and stories of leaders who self-destructed on the way up. Unless you've been living under a rock, you know their names and faces. You've seen them interviewed by nightly news anchors, you've read the scandalous articles online, and you've possibly thought, *But that could never happen to me.*

According to the *Harvard Business Review*, two out of five new CEOs fail in their first eighteen months on the job. It appears that the major reason for the failure has nothing to do with competence or knowledge or experience, but rather with hubris and ego. In other words, they thought, *But that could never happen to me.*

I'm here to tell you that it can happen to you. And if by some stretch of the imagination you believe you're immune to a crash-and-burn because of your faith in God, then you're living with the exact kind of naiveté that can ruin your reputation, your family, your health and your legacy. Your name can be added to that ever-growing pile at the bottom of the ladder of success. In my work with hundreds of leaders from across the world, I find that far too many have eagerly entered the workplace, marketplace or mission field with the goal of establishing themselves and striving toward a successful future. But unfortunately they overlooked something crucial along the way. They end up in my office soaked in tears and shame because they were fired for ethical violations, they didn't know how to work on a team, or they even succumbed to the dark allure of money, sex and power. At one time they thought, *But that could never happen to me.* But it did.

The obvious question here is, why? I'll offer my take. But I warn you, the answer is not pretty.

Dirty Little Secret

We can prostitute our very souls in our attempts to be successful. We can sell out, cave in and go morally bankrupt chasing the god of success. Knowing this perilous potential, Jesus himself warns us that we can lose our souls by too much gaining, saying, "What kind of deal is it to get everything you want but lose yourself? What could you ever trade your soul for?" (Matthew 16:26). It is no deal at all to lose our soul in striving after the goddess of success. In doing so we pay the ultimate price—a price we do not, in fact, need to pay.

That's strong language. Success as the world defines it has become a god to us. Yet the first of the Ten Commandments is "You shall have no other gods before me." We may not have put success before the Lord God, but we've sure put it alongside him. Moses feared success for his people more than he feared a life in the wilderness. He warned his people of its dangers:

> Make sure you don't forget GOD, your God, by not keeping his commandments, his rules and regulations that I command you today. Make sure that when you eat and are satisfied, build pleasant houses and settle in, see your herds and flocks flourish and more and more money come in, watch your

standard of living going up and up—make sure you don't become so full of yourself and your things that you forget GOD, your God,

the God who delivered you from Egyptian slavery;

the God who led you through that huge and fearsome wilderness,

those desolate, arid badlands crawling with fiery snakes and scorpions;

the God who gave you water gushing from hard rock;

the God who gave you manna to eat in the wilderness, something your ancestors had never heard of, in order to give you a taste of the hard life, to test you so that you would be prepared to live well in the days ahead of you.

If you start thinking to yourselves, "I did all this. And all by myself. I'm rich. It's all mine!"—well, think again. Remember that GOD, your God, gave you the strength to produce all this wealth so as to confirm the covenant that he promised to your ancestors—as it is today. (Deuteronomy 8:11-18)

Have you ever thought some of those things to yourself—those phrases that are the whisperings of success?

"I did it all, all by myself."

"Look at what I have become."

"It's all mine."

J. B. Phillips was a successful pastor and prolific author in the mid-twentieth century. He was a colleague and friend of C. S. Lewis's, and it was Lewis who personally endorsed Phillips's translation of the Bible into everyday language for modern readers. His books sold into the millions and are still popular today. Phillips's legendary success established him as a leading voice in the work of the church all around the world. But in Phillips's autobiography, *The Price of Success*, he personally laments the great cost of his worldly success. He writes:

I was in a state of some excitement throughout 1955. My work was intrinsically exciting. My health was excellent; my future prospects were rosier than my wildest dreams could suggest; applause, honor and appreciation met me everywhere I went. I was well aware of the dangers of sudden wealth and took some severe measures to make sure that, although comfortable, I should never be rich. I was not nearly so aware of the dangers of success. The subtle corrosion of character, the unconscious changing of values and the secret monstrous growth of a vastly inflated idea of myself seeped slowly into me. Vaguely I was aware of this and, like some frightful parody of St. Augustine, I prayed, "Lord, make me humble, but not yet." I can still savor the sweet and gorgeous taste of it all: the warm admiration, the sense of power, of overwhelming ability, of boundless energy and never-failing enthusiasm. It is very plain to me now why my one-man kingdom of power and glory had to stop.[1]

A one-man or one-woman kingdom of power and glory—that's the danger. That's the kind of success that leads us to forget who is behind any strength and wealth we have achieved. As we will explore in this book, what's at stake in our success is the "subtle corrosion of character, the unconscious changing of values and the secret monstrous growth of a vastly inflated idea of myself." It's not that success is inherently wrong. It's that we have allowed it to rival God and God will share his worship with no one and no thing. God is a jealous God. And we have become unfaithful spouses.

But guess what? It doesn't have to be that way.

Here's the good news. We can climb that ladder of success to live and finish well. Now does this indicate we're going to have to define exactly what "success" and "finishing well" mean? Yes, and that's a part of what this book is about. In fact, much of what is presented here will be a redefinition of such words and phrases. We tend to form our definitions of success and happiness by the world around us. We begin with childish ways of demonstrating success—the one with the most toys wins—and this attitude carries forward in life as we age, acquire more power and increase the size of the shadow we cast amongst all the other trees in the forest. But here, childish ways must be put aside. And as we put aside childish definitions of success, we will be challenged to form a more virtuous, precise and life-guiding understanding of not only success but also inner contentment and deep satisfaction.

And here's the hard news: It's going to take work, something called "the work before the work."

In the opening of part one, I shared the story of the celebrated Chinese woodcarver. What set this man apart from his peers was his decision to do the work before the work. Had he skipped this crucial step he would have been like any other woodcarver. Whether it is work before the work, work during the work, or work after the work, I call this the "Inside Job"—a process of learning, adjusting, repenting and starting anew with courageous convictions. These convictions are anchored in ancient truths lived out by ordinary folks who have assumed the helm of leadership and lived well. In the wake of their conviction and choices, they hearken to a higher calling, live with a more noble passion and experience contentment not found in mere earthly pursuits.

Nothing New

It would be tempting to think that we're the first to see such an unprecedented crisis of character—that this is some new phenomenon. But that's not true. This problem, sadly, is recorded throughout the pages of the Bible where we see men and women with undeniable promise and gifts get tripped up in unwise choices and bottom out in disgrace and dishonor.

Remember David, the warrior poet? Instead of going to war with his men he went to bed with another man's wife. The consequences were catastrophic. Or how about Barnabas, Paul's companion on many of his missionary journeys? He simply could not find a way in his heart to be a team player. The result was a tragic split in their shared leadership. And it's not just the men. The women are there too. Two women in one of Paul's first churches nearly split the church because of their uncontrolled tongues and poisoned hearts for each other. Then there's Sapphira. She and her husband could not bring themselves to make good choices with money. They fell into hoarding, a couple of misers with their God-given resources— and as a result became a negative example for all.

And don't forget Peter, that impetuous disciple who always spoke before thinking. He would be an unlikely candidate to speak about character. Or would he? Interestingly enough, based on the extraordinary writings of this apostle, I've found that we can discover the much-needed and absolutely necessary character building blocks that assure us we will "never fall" and keep us from becoming "ineffective and unproductive" (2 Peter 1:8, 10 NIV).

There's Something About Peter

Tertullian (A.D. 155–250), the early Christian historian, wrote that "Peter endured a passion like that of the Lord." Peter's name is mentioned roughly two hundred times in the New Testament. He began his vocational career as a small business owner along with his brother Andrew and their associates James and John. His fishing enterprise was abruptly cut short, perhaps in a midcareer crisis, when he met Jesus. That encounter changed everything for Peter.

Peter became one of only a handful of important eyewitnesses to the life and legacy of Jesus of Nazareth. Not only did Peter's passion change from fishing for food to shaping and discipling men and women, but Peter's own life was transformed—changed from the inside out. Perhaps this is why Peter is so concerned with the inner traits of a would-be leader and outlines for us the inner markers necessary to live successfully and finish well. Peter knows about the work before the work.

Luke, a medical doctor and the first church historian, tells us that Peter was the leader, second to none, of the rapidly spreading church. It was Peter, not Paul, who first realized that the message of Jesus was intended for people outside the Jewish faith (see Acts 10). He was a persuasive preacher, a formidable thinker about life, faith and leadership, and a passionate defender of the faith against the criticisms and persecution that threatened the expanding church. In the end, Peter was martyred for his participation in the greatest movement the world has ever known. According to legend, he was crucified upside down. The world's final assessment of him was that he got it all backward.

On the practical side, Peter was married and his wife even accompanied him on some of his journeys (1 Corinthians 9:5; 1 Peter 5:13). Peter was a family man, caring for his mother-in-law (Mark 1:29) and brother Andrew. He knew well the challenges of balancing the pressures of small business with the competing demands of family. Peter's proximity to Jesus is clearly seen in the Gospels; he was present during many of Jesus' major miracles, including his walking on water and the transfiguration. Peter's witness of the remarkable miracles of Jesus foreshadowed the miracles he himself would do later, as seen in the book of Acts. Luke tells us that Peter had such power that people scrambled to stand in his literal shadow as he walked by (see Acts 5 for this story). This kind of charisma, influence and leadership make Peter worthy of our examination. It ought to tell us something.

Every single time we see a list of the twelve disciples in the Gospels, Peter's name is first. In the New Testament church, Peter's leadership was vast and unquestioned. Evidently he was first among equals in the first-century world. Peter's journey of becoming a great leader is chronicled for us in the New Testament. And it is precisely this process of Peter's shaping as a leader that gives him the transparency, vulnerability and authenticity to speak to us today. Eugene Peterson writes:

> The way Peter handled himself in that position of power is even more impressive than the power itself. He stayed out of the center, didn't "wield" power, maintained a scrupulous subordination to Jesus. Given his charismatic personality and well-deserved position at the head, he could have easily taken over, using the prominence of his association with Jesus to promote himself. That he didn't do it, given the frequency with which spiritual leaders do exactly that, is impressive. Peter is a breath of fresh air.[2]

A breath of fresh air indeed. In Peter we see an ordinary man transformed into an exceptional influencer of men and women. His doubts were transformed into steel convictions, his humility was aligned with that of Jesus himself, and he displayed the ability to finish well in the face of suffering and persecution. We are privileged to see Peter's redefining of success. His inner transformation becomes a light that beckons us to find our own way through the swirling whitewaters we are in today.

Peter did his own Inside Job. He had to. He learned in following Jesus that the inside of a person is where the action is. Peter knew that looks can be deceiving. To integrate his outside life with his interior landscape he needed to do the work within.

Peter's Work Within the Work

In the last of Peter's letters to the New Testament church, we find an outline for the work that men and women need to do who aspire to successfully finish well. The aging, accomplished and able leader says this:

His divine power has given us everything we need for a godly life through our knowledge of him who called us by his own glory and goodness. Through these he has given us his very great and precious promises, so that through them you may participate in the divine nature, having escaped the corruption in the world caused by evil desires.

For this very reason, make every effort to add to your faith goodness; and to goodness, knowledge; and to knowledge, self-control; and to self-control, perseverance; and to perseverance, godliness; and to godliness, mutual affection; and to mutual affection, love. For if you possess these qualities in increasing measure, they will keep you from being ineffective and unproductive in your knowledge of our Lord Jesus Christ. But whoever does not have them is nearsighted and blind, forgetting that they have been cleansed from their past sins.

Therefore, my brothers and sisters, make every effort to confirm your calling and election. For if you do these things, you will never stumble, and you will receive a rich welcome into the eternal kingdom of our Lord and Savior Jesus Christ.

So I will always remind you of these things, even though you know them and are firmly established in the truth you now have. I think it is right to refresh your memory as long as I live in the tent of this body, because I know that I will soon put it aside, as our Lord Jesus Christ has made clear to me. And I will make every effort to see that after my departure you will always be able to remember these things. (2 Peter 1:3-15 NIV)

And with those words we begin our journey into the work within the work.

■ ■ ■

Let's face it. Life as we know it isn't working well for most of us anymore. We're in trouble. I don't need to quote statistics of the sad stories we read about, hear about and are eyewitnesses to every single day in the workplace. It's obvious something isn't right. But all is not lost. The Inside Job offers each of us a way to dig down deep and do the work within the work in order to move beyond surviving to experience a kind of thriving.

Perhaps you picked this book up because something intrigued you in the title or you heard about it from someone else. Well, I'm going to tell you what you may already suspect. I'm going to confirm what you may already fear. Moreover, I'm going to articulate what the angst is—the thoughts that roll around in your head as you toss and turn in the middle of the night. If we know the demons we're fighting, we have a better chance of slaying them.

First, I want to offer some language that will help identify the source of our issues regarding leadership gone bad. I'll also share true stories of toxic leadership and how some people were transformed to become better versions of themselves. These people have implemented some of the insights found in this book, and life is very different for them as a result. In particular, their work is different. They have found more contentment, more inner peace, more awareness and an awakening to their role in changing the world.

A false god to success has been built in our lifetime. With your help, I want to help tear that god down right before your eyes. In doing so, I hope to help you redefine success. I want you to define the life you really hope to live. After all, why should we climb some ladder if it leads to a place we really don't want to go?

The prolific Catholic monk Thomas Merton wrote much on the illusions of success throughout his brief life. His advice seems more timely now than when he first penned these words:

> If I had a message to my contemporaries it is surely this: Be anything you like, be madmen, drunks, and bastards of every shape and form, but at all costs avoid one thing: success. . . . If you are too obsessed with success, you will forget to live. If you have learned only how to be a success, your life has probably been wasted.[3]

Are we in danger of being so obsessed with making it that we simply forget to live? If you watch television, you know that many ads focus on saving for retirement—something surely we need to do. But isn't there a bigger goal in life than a hefty nest egg? What if we save and hoard and then get sick or die young? What if we never really live the one life we've been given to live on this extraordinary planet?

One way of redefining success is to redefine "the good life." We have to unlearn what we've been taught because we've been sold a lie. I believe you know that as well as I do. Or at least you feel it—and have perhaps felt it for a very long time.

Many of us have tried find balance time and time again. But despite our efforts to lay down all the plates we spin, it often feels like life is crashing down around us. We eventually learn that "balance" is a dead end. But if balance is a lie just like the good life is a lie, then what other paradigm can we find to help us do our work, live our lives, love our families, enjoy our friends and do our part in changing this great big world we live in?

The answer, my fellow travelers, is not that hard to understand. It's not complex, and it will not cost you thousands of dollars (which you'd probably have to put on a credit card). It lies in the reality that we've been trying to drink from busted cisterns (see Jeremiah 2:13). Our systems, our beliefs, our ladders—they're all broken and have led us to nowheresville.

We might be rich but we're lonely. We might work hard but our exhaustion is catching up to us. We're running on empty and calling this manic pursuit a life worth living. But it is not. It is not worth living and you already know this.

What I am going to tell you here has been scraped out of the hearts of thousands of leaders I have worked with in my life—men and women who are leaders either in the marketplace or in some sphere of Christian ministry. These good people hit a dead end somewhere along their journey. Some have made mistakes. Some have left massive carnage behind them. Some got stuck. Some have done something wrong—*really* wrong. They have sinned. And somehow, even after being forgiven, they still come up empty, unfulfilled, stunted and thwarted in living the life they long for deeply in their hearts. What I write here is true. I have witnessed much despair as leaders try climb the slippery, treacherous slope of success. The reality is that they're at the bottom, and it feels like hell. In fact, it hurts like hell.

Here I will confess that I was one of those who lost their way. I swallowed the pill that promised success. I drank the liquor of my profession for many years and became intoxicated in my leadership. I am a recovering workaholic. I lived life in a stupor that many of you can relate to. Life for me was about my work. It became a mistress who promised me everything but in the end delivered nothing. Now, by implementing the lessons I'm offering here, I am recovering the life I lost. It's not about looking back but going forward, about doing the work that enables me to see work, life and faith differently.

Obviously this book is for the person who knows something about Jesus and, hopefully, is a follower of the teachings of Jesus. (If you're not, I hope that when I define what faith means you'll consider what I'm saying and choose to be a follower, like me.) You may even be part of the crowd who knows a few things about "spiritual formation." Yet for all we know about this impressive-sounding phrase, many of us have not yet connected the dots between our hearts and our work, our longings and our limitations, our ceaseless efforts to find footing amidst competing demands and rival priorities. We still live in silos: God is in one, work is in another, and fun is in yet another. Of course, some of us don't even have a fun silo.

Here we will learn that there are no silos in life. Everything we do, have done and will do is connected. There is especially no such thing as a silo of our spiritual life. The spiritual life, when properly understood, is connected to our money, our workweek and our feeling of being in or out of sync. What we learned as children we will learn again as adults—the toe bone is connected to the foot bone, the foot bone is connected to the leg bone, and so on.

Here we will integrate the journeys of our vocational life, our health life, our love life and our legacy life. We will seek to be integrated in all we've learned and experienced. We want to pray like David did: "Give me an undivided heart." We want our souls to somehow be connected to our roles. We are tired of living one way at home and another way at work, what I call "role and soul confusion." The silos will need to come down—all the way down. We will explore how living an undivided life, a life that is good and feels good, comes together for us.

A Quiet Revolution

My aim here is not to raise up an army of the dissatisfied and call them to arms. This is not a call to arms. It is a call to the heart to reflect, to awaken and to practice living the life you want to live.

A quiet revolution begins when we as leaders face the interior of our lives. A revolution of any magnitude begins first within the heart. Inside the heart and deep within the soul lies the fodder for the fire. Deep within us is the space where we go to do our work— our Inside Job.

We do this interior work to build our outside lives. We lead from the place within where conviction lies, where the motivation to change something in our outside world is birthed. It is precisely in this inside space—this interior and often unexplored domain— where leadership begins. We can acquire skills. We can amass information. We can gain tips. But nothing replaces our need to do the work within the work.

When we do our Inside Job, we participate in a revolution that not only changes us; it mobilizes us to become change agents in our organizations, companies, cultures and countries. Revolutions and reformations occur when individuals awaken to truth. This awakening breeds change. Courage is birthed and a way to move forward is forged. We see things we had not envisioned before. We find a way to move outward and onward, and thus change happens one person at a time.

This book is meant for you, the individual—whatever your age, whatever your stage in leadership and wherever you find yourself right now.

It's never too late to do the Inside Job.

■■■

When I went to my doctor six months ago, I had to face myself, my DNA and my lab results squarely in the eye. Denying what the evidence was telling me would not help me. I had to wake up. First we awaken to the realities. We'll look at this process (and I'll tell more of my story) in this chapter and those that follow.

In chapter three I offer you a paradigm shift, a different way to think through your life, your work, your dark side and the years of journeying still ahead of you. Some of us new to the leadership journey may not even know we have a dark side that will "do us in" if the light is not brought to us—if it is not lighted within us. As Mary Oliver has said, "The heart has many dungeons. Bring the light! Bring the light."[4]

In part two of this book, we'll think through what it means to live not merely a successful life but a life of virtue. We will redefine success, and with this new definition we'll embark on a new journey, equipped with tools that will help us navigate the whitewater we live in. We will explore how the word "journey" is the ideal met-. aphor for us to understand this life. We will learn about rhythm. We will explore living within our limits. We will understand how to transition well from one job or place to the next. We will see the larger picture of what's happening in our lives and what to do when we hit a wall or fall off the wagon.

Part three of this book describes resilience. I will help you understand both what it looks like and what it takes to live a resilient life. We all get knocked down by the many blows dealt us in life. But how do we choose to get up again? And finally, we will explore the consuming question we all have of where to find contentment. As we live and as we lead, we hopefully learn the secret of contentment. If we don't get this lesson right, we really will pay the price of success and wallow in our earthly rewards that will not go with us beyond the grave.

It is my hope that you will join arms with a few to walk this new journey. The Bible is true when it tells us:

Two are better than one,
　　because they have a good return for their labor:
If either of them falls down,
　　one can help the other up.
But pity anyone who falls
　　and has no one to help them up.
Also, if two lie down together, they will keep warm.
　　But how can one keep warm alone?
Though one may be overpowered,
　　two can defend themselves.
A cord of three strands is not quickly broken. (Ecclesiastes
　　4:9-12 NIV)

We sharpen each other together. Alone we are dull. So if you're reading this book alone, perhaps you need to stop and ask a coworker or friend, "Would you read this with me so we can talk about it and work through some of the issues the author is raising?" It will not hurt you to do this; it will only help you. We enter the way of transformation in community and with community—never alone.

Life is good when it is shared, not when it is hoarded and we allow no one in to share the wine of our lives. It's a sad reality that we live such quiet lives of epic desperation, and we do it solo. We are lonely in crowds. We are lonely in our churches. And sadly many of us are lonely in our own homes. The good life I will describe here is a life shared—and shared with a few. It is in the few, not the many, that we finally find what Jesus told us all along: "Where two or three gather in my name, there am I with them" (Matthew 18:20 NIV).

Lastly, this book and the accompanying workbook are chock-full of examples, case studies and suggestions that do not require a degree in rocket science to understand or implement. The way I am asking you to follow is not hard. But it does require all of the above to work.

Together, we are going to participate in our own transformation. We will not get zapped. We will not have surgery. We do not need a brain transplant. We participate in our own transformation because God has given us all we need to live the way he is asking us to live. It's just that the pill, the liquor, the Kool-Aid we've swallowed has duped us into thinking that there must be something else—something more, some secret, some list of twenty-one steps we must take, some new technique withheld from us until now. That kind of thinking has only led to our dis-ease.

We have to stop thinking this way. We will shift to see how a life of work, a life of longing, and a life of choosing the right way and walking in it can converge for our own well-being and soul satisfaction. My aim in the end is to say along with David in the Psalms, "Surely your goodness and love will follow me all the days of my life" (Psalm 23:6).

But if that is to happen, there's work to be done. An Inside Job.

2

Signs of the Times

◆◆◆

Consider the words of theologian Karl Rahner:

> [The] temptation to sin . . . attacks man unexpectedly, . . . his hunger for good fortune, his sadness and the melancholy of life that lusts for an anesthetic, his trust in the concrete, his mistrust in the future of the hereafter, his amazing and uncanny facility for moral counterfeiting which can make good evil and evil good.[1]

These words are an accurate diagnosis of our culture, an apt description of the times in which you and I are living.

- *A hunger for good fortune.* We long for the outer markers of success.

- *A sadness and melancholy about life.* Ninety percent of the drugs prescribed by doctors and filled by pharmacists are mood-altering drugs.

- *Lusting for an anesthetic.* This drives a behavior of escapism, drugs, thrill seeking and so on.

- *A mistrust of the future and a search for what is concrete.* One of the marks of the millennial generation is right here.

- *The uncanny ability to counterfeit our morals.* What we once called "evil" we call good and what we once called "good" we call evil.

We live in an age where there is a heavy pursuit of what will gratify, but in the end we slowly sober up to the realization that nothing will satisfy. Peter's words sound like the tolling bells in a chapel spire, beckoning us back to our senses as they did long ago when it was time to pray, time to turn back to God, time to get our spinning world straight.[2]

Over the years we have developed a staggering ability to rationalize what is happening around us. "It's the times we live in." "We have to keep up with the times." "The only absolute anymore is change." What we used to call evil is now good. What we used to believe was unlawful is now the law of the land. In this age of tolerance and acceptance, have we made progress? Or have we lost something vital, something life-giving?

To counterfeit morals, as Rahner puts it, is to replace ancient values with new and phony ones. What's acceptable today is often a bogus form of God's ideal for us. This is precisely what the seasoned and wise Peter is telling us in 2 Peter 1. His plea is actually a warning to look up, to get a divine perspective on life before we fully embrace the changes that happen in time and through culture.

I find it interesting that Peter's list of needed virtues and qualities—faith, goodness, knowledge, self-control, perseverance, godliness, mutual affection and love—stands in contrast to what are known as the seven deadly sins—pride, anger, lust, gluttony, envy, sloth and greed. The early church fathers and mothers designated these seven sins as the primary roots from which all other sins spread. They actually sound a lot like Rahner's diagnosis of our culture:

- *Pride.* The desire for power and fame. A drive to be in charge. Image-management and cultural control to protect the persona of the leader. Being satisfied with self but no one else. Rampant in a performance culture that keeps gifted, charismatic leaders on top and pushes others less gifted to the side and in the shadows.

- *Anger.* The raw emotion of disappointment and disillusionment revealed in rage, outbursts of temper. Examples include road rage, school shootings, domestic violence, and physical, verbal and emotional abuse. Revenge is a tool used to manipulate systems, organizations and teams to conform and to stay on task—or else!

- *Lust.* The craving for more—and "more" is always shifting. To hunger and covet for what is out of bounds. Usually involves addiction, entanglements in unhealthy relationships, codependency and acting out.

- *Gluttony.* Overdoing it. Lack of self-control. About much more than physical appetite—it is the desire to continually feast but never fast from anything.

- *Envy.* The jealousy that rises up when there is a perceived inequality; in other words, when you have more than I do. The unbridled dark desires driven by want and the feelings that emerge when the want is not fulfilled.

- *Sloth.* Apathy. Summed up in the word "whatever." Living in a self-perceived powerless state that forces one to resign to a life not desired. Not engaging in effort. Not exerting one's will and refusing to ask for help to change from one's community or God.

- *Greed.* The desire for more. Often expressed in cravings that are not healthy. Bowing to the desire for *more* money, *more* power, *more* sex, *more* everything.

Sadly, these seven sins dominate the soul of many workers today both in ministry and the marketplace. For all our advancement and technological know-how you'd think we would have overcome such failings. But we haven't. Far from it! We call evil good and good evil. It is all a spin, something I refer to as "spiritual posing."

Spiritual Posing

Spiritual posing is playing a role with your soul not in it. It is wearing a mask and living from the false self rather than true identity. Spiritual posing is described allegorically in Hans Christian Andersen's fable "The Emperor's New Clothes," where the leader is obsessed with others' impressions of him and so masquerades in a false life. This posing is as old as Jesus' condemnation of the religious right in his own day—the Pharisees who looked good on the outside but whose insides revealed spiritual slime. It was fake in Jesus' day, and it is fake today. We talk the talk but do not walk the walk. We primp and preen so as to look impressive on the outside while inside we wallow in our private mess. Being fake, we live fake lives and build fake movements full of dysfunction and secrets.

In my work with churches and Christian organizations, I am often called on to consult with elders and deacons when something goes wrong inside the walls of the church. Our team was recently working at a megachurch where the senior pastor resigned under pressure, leaving the staff and church in disarray and a state of disillusionment. We listened to dozens of staff members share their stories, and the stories converged on the following shared confessions:

- "He [the senior pastor] was a control freak."
- "It was his way or the highway."
- "Over the years, I simply survived. I left my heart somewhere outside the doors of this church and I still can't find it."
- "He made me feel worthless, like a cog in his wheel."

- "He was obsessed with numbers and himself and increasing attendance at all costs."

- "I worked here seven years and never had a one-on-one with him and I'm supposed to be a 'senior leader.' It's a joke. A sad joke."

- "I was never invested in. I'm not even sure he knew my last name. I felt marginalized the entire time he was here."

This leader had exquisite speaking gifts; his image was compelling. But as you can see, he cast a shadow of dark, unhealthy leadership. As we probed further into the story, we learned that this pastor had been fired from the previous three churches where he'd served. A serial poser.

Edging God Out (EGO)

The elevation of self, or ego, is dangerous. I call this EGO—Edging God Out. It's where personality and persona are elevated above the ways of God and even above God himself. This danger, this inclination is what Peter insists on warning leaders about in 2 Peter 1. He keeps saying, "There is another way to do this. There is another way to lead. There is another way to be." Peter speaks about escaping, not embracing, the "corruption in the world." He flashes a red warning light at every aspiring leader when he speaks of "evil desires."

Peter's list of virtues in 2 Peter 1:5-7 safeguards us against a culture where moral counterfeiting seems acceptable. He doesn't want any spiritual masquerading—people who appear one way but deep down are completely another. Peter's virtues are core. They are central. They are the estuary where rivers of life meet.

They really are the core values, the building blocks of the kingdom that Jesus himself spoke of. This is the place where Jesus' Beatitudes in Matthew 5:3-13, Paul's description of love in 1 Corinthians 13:4-7, and Peter's eight essential virtues converge. These virtues are simply the sum of what it means to be a real man or a real woman—something many people long to know and experience today.

When Peter's virtues are embraced and developed, a leader is on guard from the internal seven sins. They form a wall of protection around one's integrity, one's character, one's true self. Through the fostering and growth of these eight virtues, a leader builds an internal barometer that helps warn her of threats, coercions and compromises.

We're told the human body has certain "sentinel glands." These glands serve as a guard, a protector, a wall against diseases. If the sentinel gland is affected by a certain threatening disease, then the doctor knows to heighten the battle and engage in a more all-encompassing fight for health. In much the same way, a leader's virtues function like the sentinel glands in the body. We have a bastion of protection when they are in place. Without them, we are exposed, threatened and vulnerable to posing.

This book lays the foundation for a life that is marked by satisfaction, healthy in its function, desired by those who seek to emulate it and, above all, experienced as real, attainable and authentic. What is important at this point is to gain an understanding of what has gone wrong in our experience of leadership—both in corporate America and within a Christian understanding of leadership.

The Medium Is the Message

Do you know the name Marshall McLuhan? His work in the field of communications is undisputed among media experts. He is regarded as a primary voice in the study of and the effects of media on culture. If you're not familiar with his name, chances are good you're familiar with something he said.

Since I was a communications major in college, I quickly became familiar with McLuhan's work. My adviser was an avid fan and introduced me to his writings and concepts. Above anything I learned was his famous quote: "The medium is the message." McLuhan believed that the real message of an ad, commercial or promotional material was not really the content of what one was promoting but the medium in which it was delivered.

The rise of television in the second half of the twentieth century made image all-important. We were shaped by a culture that said, "Image is everything." Looks, personality, charisma, power, wealth, glamour and beauty became more important than ever before. Success underwent a redefinition. The weight of one's character did not matter as much as the ability to look good on the screen or the printed page. That has now extended to the World Wide Web with YouTube, Instagram, Tumblr and more.

Sadly, the cult of image has infected the church as well—Christian leaders, pastors and authors. I overheard someone in an office talking about what their pastor wore as he preached. She described his pants, the cuff, his socks and belt in great detail She then exclaimed, "I know exactly where he got that outfit and my son wants one just like his." Nothing was mentioned about his message. The medium was the message. And this medium has knocked us off course—way off course.

To help us see how far off course we have veered, let's briefly look at two major biblical characters—Moses and Peter.

Was Moses a Poser?

Moses did not possess what we would consider to be the absolute must-haves in a leader. In fact, we would probably bypass him on our way to find someone who better fits our cultural mold. We're told bluntly that Moses was not a good communicator. He was not a natural orator. In fact, Moses was a reluctant leader, even arguing with God about why he should not be the one to do the tasks God desired. He told God plainly, "Master, please, I don't talk well. I've never been good with words, neither before nor after you spoke to me. I stutter and stammer" (Exodus 4:10). He was simply confessing his self-perceived inadequacies for leadership.

Elsewhere the Scriptures tell us that Moses was not charismatic: "Now the man Moses was a quietly humble man, more so than anyone living on Earth" (Numbers 12:3). When he had his dramatic experience with God through a burning bush, he was on the backside of a mountain, not in the court of the powerful Pharaoh. Perhaps he didn't even have the resources to own his own flock of sheep. The epic movies made by Hollywood about Moses show him as larger than life, a man who can do it all—anything other than how the Bible actually portrays him. Culture again has reshaped our understanding of the people God uses.

Then there's Peter. We see him enter the story of Jesus as a small business owner, an ordinary fisherman. As the story unfolds, we see him as a doubter of the truth, a powermonger who is corrected several times by Jesus, and ultimately a man who denies and betrays the one man he's been committed to in life. Yet through this apprenticeship, we see Jesus choose Peter among all the other first-century disciples to both feed and tend his flock of people. Jesus saw what was invisible to others. Jesus saw Peter's heart, his potential to become a great leader.

The book of Acts reveals a little of the private life of Peter. We know he spent time alone praying. We know that, as an older follower of Jesus, he was still subject to correction. We see his passion in his work and devotion to Jesus up until the very end of his life where according to historians he was crucified upside down.

In a world where the medium seems to shout that we need more power, more money, more control and authority, Peter offers a more hopeful perspective. He gives us a different paradigm of how to live well and lead well—and shows us that these don't have to be opposing values or experiences. By integrating the principles I am going to outline for you in this book, you can find a way to integrate your outside world with your inner world. You will be able to both live and lead from a place that is grounded in truth. Peter experienced this, and so have many other men and women who have followed this way. Peter's leadership, built on the foundation of Moses' words, welcomes us down a different path than the competitive, demanding, draining road so many leaders are trying to navigate today.

In the next chapter, we'll look at the outer markers of success that captivate our leadership culture today and compare these to the life-giving virtues that Peter encourages us to embrace.

3

COMPARING THE INNER AND OUTER MARKERS OF SUCCESS

◆◆◆

The Latin phrase *Repetitio mater studiorum est* means "Repetition is the mother of all learning." If something is really important, it bears repeating. We tell people again and again and then one last time, "Don't you forget this!" Five times in Peter's second letter we are reminded not to forget.

- "Do these things." (2 Peter 1:10 NIV)

- "I will always remind you of these things." (2 Peter 1:12 NIV)

- "I think it is right to refresh your memory." (2 Peter 1:13 NIV)

- "I will make every effort to see that after my departure you will always be able to remember these things." (2 Peter 1:15 NIV)

- "You will do well to pay attention to it." (2 Peter 1:19 NIV)

Peter is shaking us to attention so we won't miss this simple truth: Character matters. It's something he doesn't want us to forget. The English word for "character" is derived from Latin roots that mean "engrave." What is engraved deep within us is the true mark of our identity. We are more than what a person sees when they look at us or even when we view ourselves in a mirror. We are more than bones, sinew, muscles and a few vital organs. Peter reminds us that our bodies are really only a "tent." We have to look deeper. We must look within for what matters most—and what matters most is our character.

Character—invisible to the eye, impossible to hear, it is that something deep inside us that etches values, principles and ethics on our soul. Character is the right stuff, and without it we wind up with the wrong stuff when it comes to leadership. The actions we choose, the words we say, the attitude we seek to live—these are the DNA of character. It is who we are when no one sees. It is what others see displayed in our fortitude and our deliberations, which ultimately result in our actions.

Peter's words are important in today's culture because the virtues he outlines are precisely the character-rich stuff that defines a leader. It's interesting to note that when both Paul and Peter speak of qualities necessary for leading the church, they speak of attributes rooted in character, not gifts or abilities.

We don't assume character. We aren't awarded character with our diplomas. We aren't promoted into having character. And character is not a gift that some have and some don't. Character is forged within us over many seasons, in hard times and good, and through experiences both exhilarating and devastating.

Inner and Outer Markers

One of the great problems of our day is that nearly all markers of success are external. We don't look within to define success. We look outside. What size is his office? What kind of car does she drive? What neighborhood do they live in? Where did he go to school? Does she have her MBA yet? If all we have are external markers of success, we are complicit in promoting a bloodthirsty culture—one that is about domination, power and control. We speed up so we can get the validation we think we need. We become aggressive in our pursuits of making life work. We make choices and use people for our own ends. We can never truly enjoy success because if we stop, slow down or smell the roses, someone somewhere, might get ahead of us. One business executive recently confessed to me, "When one of my colleagues succeeds at something, a part of me dies. I can't be happy for her because I know I've just been bypassed." It's a sad state of the soul.

When these external markers eclipse other guiding values available to us, we become servants of success and our hearts become enslaved, one quadrant at a time, until we are dead to honor, enslaved to money and paralyzed to move in a different direction.

These aspirations to be great and to be first are as old as the stories within our Bible. It's interesting to find even the early followers of Jesus caught in plotting their own legacy so as to be remembered as one among the greats. In five short verses, Jesus shifts their paradigm and stretches their understanding of real leadership:

> They came to Capernaum. When he was safe at home, he asked them, "What were you discussing on the road?"
>
> The silence was deafening—they had been arguing with one another over who among them was greatest.
>
> He sat down and summoned the Twelve. "So you want first place? Then take the last place. Be the servant of all."
>
> He put a child in the middle of the room. Then, cradling the little one in his arms, he said, "Whoever embraces one of these children as I do embraces me, and far more than me— God who sent me." (Mark 9:33-37)

First place is last place. That's a radical shift in understanding— one enough to make the proud fall and the humble be exalted. Jesus' model of leadership was something the eager-beaver emerging leaders found difficult to grasp. Surely it would be about power.

Most certainly it would be about grandeur and greatness. Wrong! This radical new paradigm of leadership took years for the early followers of Jesus to develop and it is no different for us today. Every definition of leadership you think you already know and perhaps already embody is turned on its head.

Jesus reveals that this kind of talk is what happens when would-be leaders are left to themselves to define leadership. The same happens to us today, doesn't it? When our inner dialogue is left to itself, it's amazing the worlds we can create to rule and dominate. But Jesus does not leave them, or us, to worlds created in isolation. He breaks in, disrupting the self-talk and inner battles of comparing ourselves to others. Jesus offers his disciples both a lesson and a rebuke. The lesson comes from the vulnerability of a child and the rebuke comes when they fail to really "get" this valuable lesson on leadership.

When Jesus catches his disciples in the act and asks them about what he overheard them arguing about, they seem embarrassed to admit the true, dark nature of their discussions. We're told that the "silence was deafening" and evidently no emerging leader would 'fess up.

But Jesus flips their world on end when he redefines greatness and true leadership by offering them the face of a powerless child. Jesus picks the child up in his arms, as if accentuating its smallness and vulnerability, and says, "Anyone who wants to be first must be the very last, and the servant of all" (Mark 10:35 NIV). Obviously a small, defenseless child is no leader in their definitions of power. But the child becomes the teacher, as they often do—a symbol of leadership right before their once-blinded eyes.

To be great is to become small. To lead is not to exercise power but to embody service. Jesus was setting forth a new paradigm. But new paradigms are hard to understand, and it would take another lesson for the disciples, when they were again caught in the act. This time they were openly asking Jesus for positions of honor, grandeur and respect. Mark's Gospel again tells us that James and John were feeling entitled, as if they were in privileged proximity to Jesus. This time in harmony they ask, "Let one of us sit at your right and the other at your left in your glory" (Mark 10:37 NIV). They wrongly assume, as sometimes leaders do, that honor and position are the outer markers that really matter. Jesus again sets them straight, but this time he goes into more detail. There is no entitlement in Jesus' understanding of leadership:

> You've observed how godless rulers throw their weight around . . . and when people get a little power how quickly it goes to their heads. It's not going to be that way with you. Whoever wants to be great must become a servant. Whoever wants to be first among you must be your slave. (Mark 10:42-44)

Again, this was a new paradigm for leaders—completely different from how they were accustomed to thinking. Leadership in Jesus' head and heart did not involve allowing power to go to the head and then using it for personal advantage. Greatness is about learning to be a servant. Period.

Never, Ever Forget!

The older, mature Peter wrote to a much younger audience, "So I will always remind you of these things, even though you know them and are firmly established in the truth you now have. I think it is right to refresh your memory" (2 Peter 1:12-13 NIV). We are never, ever finished with learning about our own development, influence and potential hazards. When James and John argue about getting personal honor and esteem, it's not during their first week on the job with Jesus. We find them having this discussion two-thirds of the way into Mark's story, more than two years into their apprenticeship with Jesus. The lessons of leadership are ongoing, constantly challenging us as we experience new scenarios. This is why Peter feels the need to remind us and remind us again that inner markers are what true leadership is all about.

My son, Leighton, is a professional golf instructor. He's a member of the PGA, gives lessons and leads a local organization teaching golf to underprivileged youth. When I golf with Leighton, he's always reminding me of the hazards up ahead. "Dad, there's a huge sand trap to the right of the green. Try to stay away from it." "Dad, there's a small stream at the bottom of the hill right ahead of us. You can't see it from here so make sure you plan to place the ball before the stream or after the stream but not *in* the stream." Leighton coaches. He warns. He gives direction. How much this same kind of coaching is needed today for all kinds of leaders, and wise is the person who seeks out a coach, a guide, a more experienced leader to speak into and give shape to his or her life. This is exactly what Peter's words can be for us.

True Success in Life

We need a new understanding of what constitutes "the good life."

Although we're called "human beings," we place far too much value in ourselves as "human doings"—and a lot of doings at that. In 2 Peter 1:5-7, Peter lists eight qualities that go a long way toward being a human being. Each of the eight is an inner marker; not one of them describes a life of success built on externals. Each of Peter's building blocks finds its root in the heart of man or woman. For life to be good, we must find meaning within ourselves, not outside of ourselves. This shift in perspective is hidden work. It is the work within. No fireworks go off when this shift happens. It's a gradual turning from illusion to reality. We turn to the source of life to find the life we want. This shift takes place in the countless mundane decisions we make every single day. Character is birthed in the ordinary time and space of our lives, and if it is not birthed there, then we have nothing to draw from when we face a crisis, hit a dead end or encounter a tremendous challenge. Character grows as a little child grows—in wisdom, physical strength and favor.

When Luke wrote his biography and account of the life and work of Jesus, he noted Jesus' own spiritual formation: "And Jesus grew in wisdom and stature, and in favor with God and man" (Luke 2:52 NIV). Jesus' growth was as a whole person; he became emotionally healthy, spiritually nurturing and physically robust. When it comes to our own growth and formation, we often seek to fill in gaps and missing pieces—something that somehow escaped our grasp but that we long for in our adulthood. Some of us missed security. Some of us missed healthy emotional environments. Some of us had no mother or no father. And we seek to fill these holes in our souls through a myriad of choices. This is what turns us into who we are—what forms our character. In leadership formation, the extraordinary is birthed in the midst of the ordinary days of our lives.

A real estate agent just placed American flags in the yards of four thousand homes in our town. She'd asked for volunteers to help place the flags, which were in honor of the July Fourth holiday, and yesterday mentioned to me that one of the high school students who helped her had "the right stuff." When I asked her to elaborate, she said, "He took initiative. He knew how to organize the other high school volunteers. He assumed leadership." In fact, this real estate agent was so moved, she offered the young man a job on the spot.

"I said, 'You stand head and shoulders above your peers and I want to help you to take the next step,'" she told me. "'Do you want to make some money and help my business?'"

In this moment a leader was born. A leader was noticed. A leader was helped to the next place on his own journey. This was nothing spectacular, but it was pretty significant for this young man and for the seasoned veteran who recognized that someone had what it takes to become a solid leader.

Leadership is born in the ordinary times of our lives or it is never born at all. It becomes not a role we assume but a story we live—a story anchored in our own formation and personal growth.

The Building Blocks

Peter does not leave future leaders in the dark about the basic building blocks to effective leadership. According to 2 Peter 1:5-7, they are:

- faith
- goodness or moral excellence
- knowledge
- self-control
- perseverance
- godliness
- kindness
- love

There's no question in Peter's mind as to the value of these building blocks. He does not mince words. He sees each as essential and lists them in an order leading to a great promise: "If you possess these qualities in increasing measure, they will keep you from being ineffective and unproductive" (2 Peter 1:8 NIV). He goes on to underscore their significance by saying, "Whoever does not have them is nearsighted and blind" (2 Peter 1:9 NIV).

Step by Step

In mentioning the eight essential qualities for a leader's development, Peter makes it clear that each one of the virtues is to be added to the others. They become like steps we take one at a time. It's a progressive journey where we move toward a real and determined goal. There is a purpose. We don't pick and choose which ones we want and which seem unnecessary. Together they form the heart of a leader's character and determine how we live and what legacies we leave. These eight virtues form the "work within the work."

The work within the work is more than what we can do with our hands, head and feet. It is the movement within our hearts. Peter describes this as a process of transformation. We change within as we work without. We move from vice to virtue, from the dark side of our personalities to the light side of a way that is more like God. As we take each of Peter's steps upward, we find we become a better version of ourselves. Skip these steps—skip the work within the work—and we are simply in an unending rat race, nothing more than the proverbial hamster on the wheel that spins and spins and spins. Move too quickly through these virtues and we become the frog in the kettle who is slowly boiled to death in the rising temperature of culture.

When someone is said to be "full of vice," it's understood to mean that the person has some sort of problem. The word "vice" comes from the Latin word *vitium*, meaning "failing or defect." A vice is a moral fault, a bad habit, something corrupted and tainted. Peter's work within the work is for us to move away from the vices and embrace the virtues. We are called to a sacred shift, to move from our ruin to our glory.

A Healthy Leader Is Always a Student

A leader who leads well is a lifelong learner, always seeking to find out more about who we are now and who we are becoming. One of the failures in current leadership theory is its tendency to overlook the value of our personal stories, of examining ourselves to see what dots we can connect to help make sense of our vulnerable spots, natural tendencies and shortcomings.

In their study of leadership, Gary McIntosh and Samuel Rima have given us a worthy volume titled *Overcoming the Dark Side of Leadership: How to Be an Effective Leader by Confronting Potential Failure*.[1] The "potential failures" they discuss are all rooted in personal history. The solution? Know yourself.

"Know thyself." This ancient Greek maxim was inscribed in marble on the temple of Apollo in Greece. It was read and known by all. In our modern times, many of us have entered a quest to know business, to know medicine, to know engineering and even to know the church. But what of knowing ourselves?

Knowing yourself is critical for your own well-being as a leader but also for the benefit of the organization you serve. Sadly, many Christians love to quote what they believe is their chief purpose in life—to know God—but what of knowing self? What if we knew the story of our formation so we could live with an awareness of where our personal pitfalls in life might be? What if we realized we would always be vulnerable to certain issues or certain people? What if we could see how our own dysfunctions contributed to the dysfunction in our organizations? And to think all this lies literally right under our own nose, in our own personal story.

One senior leader of an organization told me, "I'm a mess inside and I create messes everywhere I go." What if there was a way for this leader to face his mess inside and reverse his trend of creating messes everywhere he goes? What if he could find wholeness and healing and lead from a place of health rather than brokenness?

A Brief Self-Assessment

Listed below are six areas to explore in your own history. After you explore them on your own, I would strongly suggest forming a small group of three to four peers and working again through these questions with the input of others.

Love. How did you experience love as a child? How were you celebrated apart from accomplishments, grades and achievements? How was loved expressed to you from birth to age eighteen?

Drivenness. Where is your compulsiveness rooted in your story? How did your father and mother and principal caregivers demonstrate how a person works and works well? Do you think your peers consider you to be a driven person?

Pride. Do you think there's a chance people view you as selfish? If so, have you traced these tendencies back to find their genesis? In your family of origin, how was love given and demonstrated?

Fear. Do you consider yourself a fearful person? Is fear something that drives your decisions—the fear of going bankrupt, the fear of being alone, the fear of others knowing you deeply, the fear of not being liked or respected? What value do you place on vulnerability?

Anger. How was anger modeled for you as a child? How did losing your temper play out in your history? Does anger play an ongoing role in your own story today? How do you express disapproval today in your relationships?

Codependency. Do you have a history of being manipulated or controlled by someone in your past? Name three people in your life who showed you how to be healthy in your relationships and wise in your interactions with others.

The Greatest Question

I've used this one question hundreds of times in my work with leaders and I want to encourage you to ask it of five of your colleagues. But before I tell you what the question is, I want to tell you a few things about the outcome of this question:

- People will tell you the truth in response to this question if you are a safe person—a person who will not react in an angry manner. A safe person is someone who does not judge but simply chooses to listen and take the person's response to heart.

- People will tell you the truth about your leadership when they believe you genuinely want to know and that you will value or dismiss their perspective.

- People will tell you the truth when you lead with the value of grace as much as the value of truth. By this I mean that too much truth is a hard thing to hear sometimes. Creating a culture of truth does not mean constant feedback or instant confrontation to settle wrongs. It means extending to others genuine love, care and concern. Giving grace allows people the space and time to process and muster the courage to tell you what is on their mind and heart. Jesus was described as a man who was full of grace and truth (John 1:17).

Okay, here's the question that can change your life and leadership: "What is it like to work with me?"

Ask that question and then give people the opportunity to form a response. Better yet, ask them the question and then say, "We're going to come back to this tomorrow. I'm serious. I want your answer." Ask them to write down some thoughts and be prepared to share it with you. In working with church and marketplace leaders, I've seen a great deal of good come from this question being a part of the fabric of their culture.

I first came across this question during some marriage counseling with Gwen. I have to admit that I'd never considered that question before in my marriage. I had simply assumed that I was fun to live with and to be married to. But Gwen had a different answer—an answer I was unprepared to hear. When I asked Gwen this question, I made the mistake of asking her in front of a retreat we were leading. Gwen chose to be honest and I was forced to listen. She said, "Sometimes it's fun to be married to you. Sometimes it's hard."

I liked the fun pàrt of her answer, but it was the "hard" word that led us into several very good conversations about the man I looked at in the mirror—the man Gwen had chosen to live out the rest of her life with. That same feeling might rise up in you as you begin to ask the question and listen to the answer. It takes great courage to know yourself. But asking this question puts you well on your way to knowing yourself in real, tangible and specific ways. Avoid this question and you'll continue to believe your own press—and trust me, that's not wise.

Here is that same question asked in different ways:

- What is it like to be my child?
- What is it like to be my spouse?
- What is it like to be on a team with me?
- What is it like to work for me?

Thomas à Kempis said, "A humble self-knowledge is a surer way to God than a search after learning."

The Inside Job Is Ongoing

Maybe you recall the story of David, the king of Israel, and his affair with Bathsheba (if not, see 2 Samuel 11). Interestingly enough, the affair did not happen when David was a young man but rather in the middle of his life. David stopped doing the work within the work; he failed to continue his Inside Job. David took another man's wife and then manipulated a massive cover-up to hide what he had done—an action that resulted in the death of Bathsheba's husband. The "man after God's own heart" ignored the work within the work and fell into a snare that caused pain for himself and many others.

From this low point David wrote the poem known as Psalm 51. His poignant words are relevant for our discussion. David articulates for us the depths of our need to get things right—with God

and with each other. Like David, we're never finished doing the
Inside Job.

> Generous in love—God, give grace!
> > Huge in mercy—wipe out my bad record.
> Scrub away my guilt,
> > soak out my sins in your laundry.
> I know how bad I've been;
> > my sins are staring me down.
> You're the One I've violated, and you've seen
> > it all, seen the full extent of my evil.
> You have all the facts before you;
> > whatever you decide about me is fair.
> I've been out of step with you for a long time,
> > in the wrong since before I was born.
> What you're after is truth from the inside out.
> > Enter me, then; conceive a new, true life.
> Soak me in your laundry and I'll come out clean,
> > scrub me and I'll have a snow-white life.
> Tune me in to foot-tapping songs,
> > set these once-broken bones to dancing.
> Don't look too close for blemishes,
> > give me a clean bill of health.
> God, make a fresh start in me,
> > shape a Genesis week from the chaos of my life.
> Don't throw me out with the trash,
> > or fail to breathe holiness in me.
> Bring me back from gray exile,
> > put a fresh wind in my sails!
> Give me a job teaching rebels your ways
> > so the lost can find their way home.
> Commute my death sentence, God, my salvation God,

and I'll sing anthems to your life-giving ways.
Unbutton my lips, dear God;
    I'll let loose with your praise.
Going through the motions doesn't please you,
    a flawless performance is nothing to you. (Psalm 51:1-16)

As we age and our leadership matures and develops, the outer markers of success can change. The things we felt were important at age thirty seem to morph. Values erode. There's a place near our retreat center where an entire mountainside has eroded. The property next door wasn't cared for well; it was overgrazed by livestock and never reseeded. Through time and in time, the topsoil all washed down into the valley.

Unless we continue to do what we know—repeat: what we *know*—to be true, erosion will happen in our heart. We drift. We become complacent. We ignore the threat within. Like David, we find ourselves doing things we vowed to never do. We lower our guard because we're tired. We live with little margin. We feel spread too thin, like we're living on fumes. And then—*boom!* What we thought would never happen happens—and it happens to us.

The good news here is that if this has been a part of your own story, you're not finished. Failure does not have to define you. You don't have to be labeled as a victim. Just as Peter was not defined by his failures, we don't have to be defined by ours. I like that!

Consider Peter and his clay feet, fledgling faith and embarrassing betrayal. But Peter is not defined by his mistakes. As we find Peter at the end of his life writing 2 Peter, he is the leader of the entire movement begun by Jesus. He is the senior leader shaped by failure and grace. We see in Peter's life and legacy that mistakes are redeemed, failures are leveraged into strengths, and shortcomings are atoned for not only in the life to come but the here and now.

As you will learn, I've failed in both my life and leadership. What is true is this: By embracing Peter's virtues, we find a way to move through our failures just as the caterpillar moves through the cocoon to emerge changed and transformed.

The Inside Job may mean for some of us a new beginning with a new commitment to live well and lead well. Like David, we want a fresh start. We want fresh wind in our sails. We want to do more than go through the motions in our work. As we stay focused on our own Inside Job and do the work within, Peter is telling us that we can not only stay the course but that we'll experience a deep satisfaction that is fulfilling, satisfying and rewarding! As Thomas Merton said, "He who fails well is better than he who succeeds badly."

Peter's Call for Effort and Work

Peter tells us to "make every effort." Character doesn't just happen. We participate in our own transformation. We choose to sit on the wheel of the divine potter and be pinched here and pressed there. Like malleable clay, we allow our heart, character and soul to be shaped through time and in time into the heart, character and soul of a leader. But we have a role to play. To make the effort requires passion, determination, commitment and seriousness. These themes will unfold in the pages of this book as we continue our understanding of how we are made and shaped.

In other words, effective leadership doesn't just happen. We grow it like a garden. We hoe the rows and weed out the weeds if we expect to gain a harvest. We learn. We apply. We implement. We evaluate. We improve. We become productive and we become efficient. As we work to develop character we experience the fruit. We lead in a different way, and we live in a different way.

It is more than a bit interesting that the root definition of the English word "virtue" is actually "manliness." It's where we get our word "virile." Before my women readers get too upset, let me say that virtue is what makes a real man *and* a real woman. Virtues are not ideals conceived by someone who sat around and thought them up. Virtues are shadow images that we find in God. All of Peter's virtues are found in the DNA of God: a God that is good, all-knowing, patient and not reactionary, pure, kind and loving. Since we are created in the image of God, we have the indelible imprinting in our souls to become like God. To embrace Peter's virtues is to embark on the journey of becoming a better version of yourself—a version that resembles God. A good God created men and women to be good people. It's that simple.

Our culture, and some popular Christian literature, espouse the view that to be a man is to be wild, to reek with testosterone, to be powerful and fierce. And to be a woman is to be physically beautiful and busty. Take a look at the men's journals and women's magazines available on our newsstands. Look at the covers. There you see in airbrushed perfection our culture's images of maleness and femaleness: men with a six-pack and women with lipstick and cleavage. But Peter is after something far more core to what it really means to be a man or woman in God's view.

In part two, we will focus on the journey each of us experiences in our life, faith and leadership formation. We will discover a language we can share as we move through life and take on different leadership roles. We'll also look in depth at the eight virtues. These eight virtues become our work within the work no matter where we find ourselves on the journey. These eight virtues build a platform for us to live and lead well. By working to develop these virtues we find a way through the chaos of our times. They come with Peter's promise—"If you do these things [uphold and practice these virtues], you will never stumble" (2 Peter 1:10 NIV). By practicing these eight virtues we are invited to participate in what Peter calls the "divine nature." When we live by these guiding principles, we're not just men and women but people who possess sacred and divine-like qualities.

Part Two

DOING THE WORK WITHIN THE WORK

◆

NOW THAT WE HAVE LOOKED at the crisis going on in today's world regarding leadership, we are ready to do the work within the work. Life is not just about our work—our jobs. We must look deeper. We need to look within. As we look within our own souls, we discover the interior landscape where true leadership is born and developed. This is an inner journey—a journey I will describe in chapter four. To know where we are headed in our leadership development is to gain a bigger picture—something like the thirty-thousand-foot view we see while cruising in an airplane. In chapters five and six we will explore the eight needed virtues and see why a leader who leads with virtues and not just a thirst for power, position and success is indeed a real leader.

In chapters seven, eight and nine we will encounter a new paradigm of how to lead and live well. Through embracing rhythm instead of balance in life, we will find a key that unlocks a door for us to embrace our own well-being as well as our leadership. When we learn more about our limits, we learn to surrender the illusions

of doing everything we think we should and relax in doing what we
can. There's a big difference. As we explore transitions, we'll discover why our endings and beginnings are so rough in life. By understanding transitions, we are given a whole new way to look at
the many changes that come our way as leaders—both personally
and in our organizations.

4

MAPPING THE JOURNEY

◆◆◆

Go into any large mall or shopping district and you are likely to find a map that displays where the stores, restaurants and shops are located. To help you get oriented, a large colored arrow points precisely to your location—"You are here!" Once you find where you are, then you know what steps to take to find your destination. Unfortunately there isn't any such map for the long, arduous journey called life. There isn't one for your vocational journey either. But there are some landmarks, or predictable stages and phases, of our adult journey for guidance. Several well-known and respected people have helped us here.[1] When we wed human developmental theories with our formation of faith and also our work journey, we find anticipated stages and phases along life's way.[2]

Augustine, an early church father, wrote in the first few pages of his *Confessions*, "God created us for a relationship with him and our hearts are restless until we find our rest in God." In short, restless hearts are on a journey—a journey to find not only rest, but significance, success, meaning and purpose. Restlessness is rampant in the workplace and ministry these days. What's next for me? What job is right? The American poet Mary Oliver challenges our restlessness this way:

Tell me, what is it you plan to do
with your one wild and precious life?[3]

Your answer to this question will obviously influence your journey ahead.

From birth to death, all of us are on this journey. As you may recall, the men and women who first followed Jesus were not called Christians. They called themselves followers of the Way. They carried the broad understanding that when one follows Jesus, one follows a pattern, a way of life. It includes failures as well as successes, following as well as leading, and embracing humility rather than elevating one's self in perpetual self-promotion. This way had predictable obstacles, expected problems, and assumed challenges for the first believers. In understanding the journey ahead, they found themselves better equipped to face the challenges that met them. They embraced the journey—just as the psalmist did when he wrote, "Blessed are those whose strength is in you, whose hearts are set on pilgrimage" (Psalm 84:5 NIV).

When we embrace "journey"—when we set our hearts on pilgrimage and accept that life and work as well as faith and relationships are all a part of that journey—we can relax from trying to figure life out. We take life as it comes. We submit to the fact that we are not in control of our lives but God is and we learn to trust God's wisdom, will and future. I cannot have the wisdom of a seventy-year-old woman I admire when I'm only twenty-five. Life teaches us much in each decade and we find meaning, purpose and resilience in every stage and phrase we journey through.

We learn to give up and surrender our rights to control the future ourselves. We gradually lay down our initiatives to become strategic and perhaps even "purpose driven." We find ourselves weary from all of the years spent trying to be productive and we just want to do something meaningful, so we say "no" to things as they've been. We grow to value the Jewish preacher who simply said, "There is a time for everything," but we also realize he did not say, "We can have it all, and have it all now." No, there are seasons, stages and phases that every man and woman in the twenty-first century will have to learn to navigate.

So to journey well is to live well. It is to accept the realities mentioned above and become more and more accepting of the interruptions, the uninvited and perhaps even unwanted events that come and seem to initially block our path.

The Language We Use

Bill recently shared the story of how his vocational journey was interrupted when he received notice that he was going to be laid off from his job. It was nothing Bill planned, wanted or invited. But that season of not having a job opened the way for Bill to do some soul-searching about what he really wanted to do with his life. He changed the trajectory of his life and started a small business in an area he was passionate about. Bill now says being laid off was one of the best things that ever happened to him. He started a new journey that also involved attending a local church and was stunned on his first visit as he heard the pastor deliver a sermon based on this verse: "And we know that in all things God works for the good of those who love him, who have been called according to his purpose" (Romans 8:28 NIV).

In using the language of journey we have a way to tell our story. We can share where we have been, where we are headed and what has happened to us and in us along the way. These categories help fellow travelers become our companions. We learn to share the way together. We build community with those who find themselves in the same season as us and encourage those who are behind us in life's journey. Those who are ahead of us will hopefully extend a hand to us and in doing so we receive strength and hope. All of this assuages the aloneness we often feel along the way.

The writer of the book of Numbers tells us that God told Moses to record "the stages in their journey" (Numbers 33:2 NIV) of the nation of Israel's wilderness experience. What follows in that book are forty places that Moses describes as the "stages of their journey." This journey took them into a wilderness wandering that lasted forty years. Wilderness is an apt description for many of us on particular parts of our journey. For example, Phil told me at one point that he'd been in a "vocational wilderness" for the past fifteen years. He tried on jobs like you might try on clothes. Nothing seemed to fit. Mary shared with me that her marriage had been a wilderness for more than ten years. Her husband had several affairs in those wandering years. She was left heartbroken and soul-sick, choosing to forgive him each time until finally she said, "I came to the dead end."

Help Along the Way

Think of it! We can find comfort right now and right here—no matter where we find ourselves on the journey. As we realize that the journey we're on is being guided by a God who is personal and not detached from our world, we are helped. We find a respite in the realization that God cares. We get to rest along the way. It's not all uphill. There are seasons and mountaintops we can thoroughly enjoy. There are also deserts and dry times we have to endure. Of all the doctrines of the Christian faith, perhaps the most staggering is simply this: we matter. Our journeys matter to God. Like the characters we read about in the Scriptures who also journeyed through challenging times, we find that we are not alone and that what we are going through is something God is indeed interested in.

Many of the men and women in Scripture realized what we will realize. Whether it is Joseph in prison, Jonah in the whale's belly or Daniel in the lion's den, they mattered, and we come away realizing that we matter too. We discover in hitting a wall that there is something better on the other side. We learn that life has not ended when we get fired or our spouse dies. It's different. Yes, it's different, and by understanding some of the predictable journey that you and I are on, we gain a sense of relief that there really is a path we trek in life.

I worked with Nick to help him understand his journey. Successful in business, Nick was reeling from the result of working too many long hours, giving his heart to his work and the leftovers to his spouse. When Nick and his wife came to us, they both realized the devastation and space that had grown between them during their thirty years together. Jan said, "We got lost somewhere along the way."

It was a true confession, and it was language that helped them clearly understand what had happened to them. They had taken separate paths and invested their hearts in their respective professions. Life happened. They each changed—and after changing, they realized that they barely knew each other anymore. We directed their time by helping them really listen to the other's story. In listening deeply they found compassion for each other. And eventually, forgiveness came through tears and realizations and awakening.

Another executive pastor came to our retreat and said, "My wife and I are roommates. We are business partners and ministry colleagues. We've lost the fire and passion; can you help us?" Marriage counseling certainly helps, but most often the leaders I sit with need something more than counseling or working through a particular issue. They need to do the Inside Job. Each of them needs to do the work within the work, and this is never accomplished in just three sessions. We need to do our own work—our Inside Job—at each season and stage of life.

If we don't have a map and the language of journey, we can easily believe the lie that success and inner contentment will magically happen when we get the right job or find the right person. At least, we'll believe the lie until we start running into the reality. And if we're not careful, we'll keep replaying that scenario for years, chasing after the magic. But it doesn't have to be that way.

In an amazing guide titled *The Critical Journey* by Hagberg and Guleich, we find six predictable stages of our journey.[4] I've taken the authors' work and combined it with my own understanding of not only our spiritual journey but our vocational journey as well, to help trace the stages of our life and work. I've also included a way to chart your own leadership journey. My hope is that this provides some language you find helpful to both identify and then articulate more clearly where you are and what you need at this particular season of life. By thinking through these categories, you can articulate where you are on the journey and then gain an understanding of what lies ahead—the work you're going to need to do to continue to grow and mature.

The six stages are:

- *The recognition of God (stage one).* This is the stage when we discover faith. We become a follower of Jesus. Our salvation happens. We develop an awareness that life is not just about us; we are part of a larger story—and we are not the lead character.

- *The life of discipleship (stage two).* This stage is a season of spiritual growth, learning and training. We are exposed to doctrine and are involved in Bible study.

- *The productive life (stage three).* We are working hard. We are producing fruit. We are serving and giving. We are of moving up the ladder. We are very goal-driven.

The wall. Hitting a wall is facing a dead-end in life—perhaps even in our faith. Something falls apart. We become exhausted with our productivity. We live with dissonance—that gnawing inner feeling of discord, of being out of sync. We may become disillusioned with our company or our church, wondering, "Is this all there is?"

- *The inward journey (stage four).* This is the season when we do our work within. It is a time of rediscovery and epiphany. It is waking up to the realization that there is more to life, work and faith—but we never knew it before. A deep integration begins to take place of faith and life with God, and this is deeply satisfying and exciting. We discover our own worth—our belovedness. We understand our identity and there is an inner transformation that results in a new outer journey.

- *The outer journey (stage five).* In this season, a true paradigm shift compels us to change our motivation for work and our view of life. Life becomes more about serving and giving. Our intentions are refined and we feel a sense of integration between our roles and our souls. We discover, in Frederick Buechner's words, that place of "deep gladness converging with the world's deepest needs."

- *The journey of love (stage six).* This is the stage in which we see ourselves as a container of love and our goal becomes to love unselfishly—even unconditionally. We die to self and begin to live for greater, more altruistic reasons. We will explore this more in the final chapter, but for now envision the most loving person you've ever known in your life—the most giving and unselfish, perhaps the one person in life who was the most "for" you—and you get a glimpse of this stage. Unfortunately very few in life dwell here.

Do you see yourself somewhere in one of those stages? Here's a diagram that will help you visualize the journey:

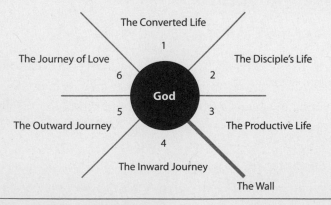

Figure 1. Stages of faith and spiritual formation

What's important to understand in this approach to the journey
is the inevitability of the wall. It's real and unavoidable. It's something that brings us to our knees. It's something so massive we
simply can't imagine going forward and perhaps don't even want to
anymore. In stages one, two and three of our journey—before we
hit the wall—life is about:

- productivity and performance—doing
- being right
- competition and achievement
- growing outwardly
- independence
- using many words and having many opinions
- stress.

Life on the other side of the wall shifts us to a new paradigm. Stages
four, five and six—otherwise known as life after the wall—are about:

- being, not just doing
- dependence, not just independence
- listening and using fewer words
- relinquishing the need to be right and hold strong opinions
- integration of our role and soul, heart and passion; moving
  toward a life we really want
- inner peace and a sense of shalom—the good life
- wanting to experience the richness of our lives and the lives of
  others.

The Leadership Journey

As you know, we don't arrive on the scene at our first jobs as great
and effective leaders. We learn along the way. Each boss becomes

.a mentor in one way or another. Each team member is a companion, and each up and down and curve offers us insight. If we're willing, we can gain valuable experience and mature, grow and develop. This is the leadership journey. Let me offer an understanding of the leadership journey that can give us language to explore where we find ourselves on the journey.

Emerging leadership (the decade of our twenties). This is when we leave college or trade school and begin our first of everything: first job, first boss, first team, first paycheck. Here everything is new. Everything is different and everything moves fast. There's a whole new kind of education going on in our lives, and our thinking sounds something like this: *Do I really like doing this? Have I made a mistake? How can I find something else?* We are green and we exchange book learning for experience—that highly valued commodity emerging leaders need and want. We may marry in this stage. We may buy a home and car and acquire real debt that brings other dynamics into this life stage.

Scaling leadership (the decades of our thirties and forties). This season is when we find ourselves scaling some sort of ladder in work and life. We are searching for more of practically everything: more money, more house, more power, more sales, more leadership, more influence. Like the Boy Scouts, we are motivated by merit badges, trips and bonuses. It's also when we may start a family and have the added pressures of babies and small children. We may move several times and have two to three jobs, each lasting a few years. These are also major years of upheaval and deep questions that surface within the leader: *Why do I feel so stuck? Isn't there something more?* It's the midlife crisis. And as the word "crisis" implies, this is a time of dangerous opportunity; we need wisdom, counsel and sound advice.

Converging leadership (the decade of our fifties). This is when our education and training, life experience, spiritual giftedness and current opportunities finally begin to converge into a flow—our "prime" years of work and life. We realize that we have paid our dues and now get to really work and serve in major roles that bring influence, significance and responsibility. In these important converging years we might discover for the first time why we were made. In this stage we often find ourselves sandwiched between aging parents and children leaving home for college or work. There is growing pressure within and without that needs to be navigated.

Kenosis leadership (the decade of our sixties). This is when we experience the internal paradoxes of regret and desire, remembering and anticipating, holding on and letting go. It is also when all we have worked for begins to cast its shadow on our lives. Our reputation is set and our character is formed. These vocational years are some of the most rewarding in that we now understand what real success looks and feels like, but we also begin to lament the brevity of time in the journey ahead.

The word "kenosis" means "to empty oneself; to be self-giving; to sacrifice."[5] It also implies a waning, as in the phases of the moon. This is essential to understand because in this important phase of our journey we have much to give back and to give to. We have learned many of the hard lessons along the way, and we are proving ourselves to be wise in spirit and action. With this wisdom comes a longing to help others avoid the mistakes we made.

Between each of these stages and phases are times of transition. I will celebrate my sixtieth birthday this year. Trust me, I've anticipated this mile marker in my own journey for a long time. As I see myself transitioning to the next phase of leadership—the kenosis stage—I feel as if the best years are ahead of me. I have something to say. I have people who actually want to hear what I'm saying, and there is renewed wind in my sails to finish well. To aid me in my new stage of life, I've planned a sabbatical. This will be a season of reflecting, resting and retooling for the next phase of my journey.

My wife and I are planning now what we want to do in this antici-pated season of ceasing—the literal meaning of the word "sab-batical." I'll talk more about the sabbatical in chapter seven.[6]

Doing the Work Within the Work

At each stage of our journey there is work to be done, both within us and outside of us. Unfortunately, our culture shapes us far more than we shape the culture. Let me be clear. The work we engage in is both slow and deep. Our culture speaks fast and shallow. We want change quickly, but quick fixes lead to what I call "pseudo-transformation"—they are an inch deep and will not last. Authentic transformation requires a slow, steady and practiced effort to allow old ways to fall away, broken patterns to be redeemed, and shelved desires to resurface. The work within the work is not a program. It is not a series of 101-, 201- and 301-level classes that we might enroll in at the university. It is on-the-job training, more caught than taught. How do you teach someone about character? How do you take a class on integrity? How do you learn about any of the eight virtues from 2 Peter 1?

Pierre Teilhard de Chardin (1881–1955) was a brilliant scientist and theologian whose work is well known in both fields. He was a paleontologist, a world-renowned geologist and a Jesuit priest. His poem "Patient Trust" reveals the slowness I am describing, which on the surface appears to be countercultural and also counter-intuitive. But it is not.

Above all, trust in the slow work of God
We are quite naturally impatient in everything
to reach the end without delay.
We should like to skip the intermediate stages,
We are impatient of being on the way to do something
unknown, something new.

And yet it is the law of all progress
that it is made by passing through
some stages of instability—
and that it may take a very long time.
And so I think it is with you;
your ideas mature gradually—let them grow,
let them shape themselves, without undue haste.
Don't try to force them on,
as though you could be today what time
(that is to say, grace and circumstances
acting on your own good will)
will make of you tomorrow.
Only God could say what this new spirit
gradually forming within you will be.
Give our Lord the benefit of believing
that his hand is leading you,
and accept the anxiety of feeling yourself
in suspense and incomplete.[7]

The only way through the stages of the journey is through them.
You can't rush the process; as much as you might want to, you can't.
Life takes time—it's a lesson we all have to learn.

5

The Great Eight Virtues, Part One

*Faith, Goodness, Knowledge
and Self-Control*

Picture a flowing river fed by winding tributaries and converging mightly into a cascading waterfall. Our virtues form the river where all of the tributaries of our character, experience, opportunity and leadership development become the waterfall. Each virtue contributes to and informs the next one on Peter's insightful and wise list:

> For this very reason, make every effort to add to your faith goodness; and to goodness, knowledge; and to knowledge, self-control; and to self-control, perseverance; and to perseverance, godliness; and to godliness, mutual affection; and to mutual affection, love. (2 Peter 1:5-7 NIV)

It's important to keep several things in mind as we explore each of the virtues in the course of this chapter and the next. First, this is not a shopping list for us to decide what we want and what we may not need. Each one is essential. Each one is invaluable in the shaping and making of a leader. None are arbitrary or optional. All are necessary in the healthy flow of effective leadership. We don't jettison one for the opportunity to pick up another. Character doesn't work that way.

Second, how we lead has to do with how we treat others. Virtues get their vertical orientation from God above, but they have horizontal implications. They flesh themselves out in our relationships with others. Virtues are not just about who we are but how we treat those around us. Notice Peter's list. Kindness and love are just as important as being able to make decisions, project growth and manage during a recession. How you lead is about the way you lead, not just that you can lead. Peter's virtues give us clearly defined areas for us to grow in as we lead.

Third, notice how each virtue is really about our behavior. The virtues are not a belief system—even the virtue of faith as I describe it is a call to action, a call to be a certain type of person who follows a certain way of life laid out for us through the teachings and example of Jesus Christ. It is not enough to simply believe to be a follower of Jesus. We are called not only to believe but to change. In fact, to change and to change often is perhaps one of the greatest callings that Jesus offers us as men and women. Trust me, being a leader in any arena will force you to be open to not only changing but growing, and this is precisely Peter's intention for us as emerging leaders or leaders in midlife.

With these parameters, let's get started. The first of Peter's virtues is faith.

Faith

Author Max De Pree has written, "The first responsibility of a leader is to define reality."[1] And being a leader, Peter begins his list of eight essential qualities with the one we must embrace to distinguish ourselves, the one that captures us with a message that is truly not our own—faith. This reality is the primary building block for everything that follows.

Currently there are more than 44,000 different Christian denominations in the United States alone, all trying to define what "faith" means and seeking to point to the essentials of belief. It's embarrassing and humbling to realize there are so many schisms, splinters and sects holding to their own versions of faith. Here I will perhaps please some or offend all, but let me try to explain what I believe Peter intended.

First, we need to understand that Jesus Christ was not a "Christian." In fact, it's clear from the four eyewitness accounts of Jesus' life and teachings that he never intended to start a new religion. He came to usher in a new way of living. The first men and women who followed Jesus at his own invitation were not called "Christians." That title came later. Initially they were called followers of "the Way" (see Acts 9:2; 19:9, 23; 22:4; 24:14, 22). And the way Jesus signaled his followers to walk was something far, far different from the rival religions of his day. Jesus called people to follow him, not the rules and regulations of a religious system.

Jesus' new paradigm for living was based on developing intimacy with God and a radical new way of relating with other people. He upheld the dignity of all human beings and maintained that all people should be recognized as image bearers of God. As the early followers of Jesus spent time together, they learned how different the way of Jesus actually was. It was new language, new methods and new shifts in their minds and hearts. It was a completely new orientation that Jesus offered in a thirty-six-month apprenticeship crash course. And it turned their world upside down.

Membership in a church is far different from being a follower of the way of Jesus. In fact, Jesus never mentioned membership in any organization. He spoke about new ways of living. He cast the vision of a new paradigm of life by describing a kingdom—an actual, unseen sphere of life that was breaking in on our reality. This kingdom is here, now and available; it's not just waiting on us after we die. We taste, sense and experience this kingdom right now. The kingdom Jesus describes has no borders. It invades the space of one's heart as much as it does one's workplace. It is focused both on one's inner world and outer actions. Jesus is after integration of these inner and outer worlds, not just saving us from our sins. Our actions, our character and our thoughts all need to be saved. This new way of thinking and living was crucial to Jesus' way.

To walk in the way is more than managing sins or bad habits. To walk in the way is to walk toward transformation—toward change at the DNA level of our souls. Hope is found in the reality that the way of Jesus is all about second chances. It's about being lost—then finding the way back. It's about inside-out change. It is truly the work within the work. This faith work is the foundational plank in our platform for building a good life—even a successful life. This faith is more action than belief, more passion than liturgy, more personal than corporate, more ethos than institution, more movement than religion.

To have faith is to begin the journey of change. Faith is a belief that there is a way and that we can walk in this way. Let me be clear. As a follower of Jesus, I am not advocating that we throw out doctrine, statements of faith and sets of beliefs. But I am urging us to think about integrating our faith into our work and not to build silos, putting work into one and faith into another. In Jesus' way of life, everything is connected. We can't be one way at work and another at home. No, a transformed life is a life of integration where we live undivided and everything comes together.

Bill came to me because he got caught in a motel room with a prostitute. Bill was a leader at work and in his church. But he realized at this point of crisis that there was something very wrong in his life, especially in light of his faith. We spent time together talking through Bill's silos of understanding and, in time, he came to realize that his sexual life mattered and that he needed to understand why he had done what he had—what he was really longing for and how his sexual abuse as a child impacted his sexual choices as a man. It was and continues to be a major part of Bill's faith journey.

Everything matters. And in the words of Flannery O'Conner, "Jesus throws everything off balance." Jesus will upset every apple cart, every temple table, every surface response, every false motivation and every private longing we ignore in our hearts. The ways of Jesus will make us examine every area of our lives. It's that simple and it's that challenging.

Goodness

Consider these words from C. S. Lewis:

> When a man is getting better he understands more and more clearly the evil that is still left in him. When a man is getting worse he understands his own badness less and less. A moderately bad man knows he is not very good: a thoroughly bad man thinks he is all right. This is common sense, really. You understand sleep when you are awake, not while you are sleeping. You can see mistakes in arithmetic when your mind is working properly: while you are making them you cannot see them. You can understand the nature of drunkenness when you are sober, not when you are drunk. Good people know about both good and evil: bad people do not know about either.[2]

Goodness is moral excellence. Goodness is not mere behavior. While it is true that "all have sinned," it is also true that there are some remarkable people in this world who are truly good. Peter welcomes everyone—sinner and saint—to continue in morals that are noble, excellent and birthed from our God, who is truly good.

Peter's appeal for goodness is at the core of the soul at work and the soul at home. Becoming a good person truly is an Inside Job—a job that requires some morphing in us, some change from the inside out. As we do the Inside Job, the outside work makes more sense. Goodness is possessing "moral excellence," as one translation puts it. Becoming good or becoming morally excellent is being good on the inside as well as the outside. When we begin the journey of following Jesus, we begin the journey of transformation of becoming good at the core. I like to say it this way—when you follow the ways of Jesus, you become a better version of yourself.

Goodness is a virtue that casts its shadow everywhere. Goodness has a way of spreading its own influence. People stop. People pause. People reflect when they experience the goodness of a teller at the bank or a taxi driver in a crowded city. Think about the last time you stopped and said, "Now that's good!" Who or what were you talking about?

I want to draw your attention to the Beatitudes, those short statements Jesus offers us in Matthew 5. Here Jesus redefines our understanding of what goodness looks, feels and acts like, of what a person who is good in heart looks like in action. This new paradigm from Jesus, which Peter encountered as an eyewitness, is about the posture of one's heart—a posture that reveals itself in action toward others. Let's look at these verses straight from the mouth of Jesus that describe the kind of person he wants us to become. Notice how truly countercultural they are. As you read, feel free to substitute "You're good" for "You're blessed":

> "You're blessed when you're at the end of your rope. With less
> of you there is more of God and his rule.
>
> "You're blessed when you feel you've lost what is most dear
> to you. Only then can you be embraced by the One most dear
> to you.

"You're blessed when you're content with just who you are—no more, no less. That's the moment you find yourselves proud owners of everything that can't be bought.

"You're blessed when you've worked up a good appetite for God. He's food and drink in the best meal you'll ever eat.

"You're blessed when you care. At the moment of being 'care-full,' you find yourselves cared for.

"You're blessed when you get your inside world—your mind and heart—put right. Then you can see God in the outside world.

"You're blessed when you can show people how to cooperate instead of compete or fight. That's when you discover who you really are, and your place in God's family.

"You're blessed when your commitment to God provokes persecution. The persecution drives you even deeper into God's kingdom.

"Not only that—count yourselves blessed every time people put you down or throw you out or speak lies about you to discredit me. What it means is that the truth is too close for comfort and they are uncomfortable. You can be glad when that happens—give a cheer, even!—for though they don't like it, I do! And all heaven applauds. And know that you are in good company. My prophets and witnesses have always gotten into this kind of trouble." (Matthew 5:3-11)

Not the way our culture, or even most churches, define goodness, is it? It is nothing less than a complete revolution in how we define goodness and become a better version of ourselves. Jesus' words, expanded on by Peter in his virtues, have some legs to them. Goodness reveals itself in the incarnate ways we live and lead. We move through this world as the ones called out to be good and to do good. In Peter's sermon to the early church in Acts 10, he distills the entire life and work of Jesus into this simple phrase: "He went around doing good" (Acts 10:38 NIV).

A good God does good things, and it follows that a good leader does good things too! Peter is reminding us that the core of leadership is leading with moral excellence and being a person who exudes in action that which is uniquely good and helpful.

Do you know people you would say are really good people? I sure do. Tim is one of them. His goodness is displayed in being trustworthy. He is a man of his word. Tim tells me he is going to do something or has done something, and I can be sure that he actually has. Tim is a good person to be friends with. Our conversations are reciprocal, not just about him. He asks me questions, probes at my heart and takes initiative with me. I'm not the one always calling him. As I watch Tim living out his life, I can see that he is a good husband—frequently talking to me about his wife and the time they've spent together or need to spend together. He's also a good father who is emotionally present to his kids. He spends time with them individually and does not try to parent "en masse." His goodness is displayed in his work ethic, the moral choices he makes about temptation he faces and more. His goodness is contagious. He makes me want to be a better person. And that is one of the true hallmarks of good people—being around them makes you want to be a better person.

Knowledge

Peter's third virtue that we are encouraged to embrace is knowledge. But knowledge of what? Education alone does not ensure that one's personal character is changed at the core. Some of the brightest people today are lured into doing unthinkable things. The amassing of information does not result in one's transformation. Peter is speaking of another kind of knowing.

Solomon, the son of the famous King David, was said to be the wisest man who ever lived—a man who had knowledge about the things of God and about life. When God told Solomon that he would give him anything he asked for, Solomon said this:

> "Here's what I want: Give me a God-listening heart so I can lead your people well, discerning the difference between good and evil. For who on their own is capable of leading your glorious people?"

God, the Master, was delighted with Solomon's response. And God said to him, "Because you have asked for this and haven't grasped after a long life, or riches, or the doom of your enemies, but you have asked for the ability to lead and govern well, I'll give you what you've asked for—I'm giving you a wise and mature heart. There's never been one like you before; and there'll be no one after. As a bonus, I'm giving you both the wealth and glory you didn't ask for—there's not a king anywhere who will come up to your mark. And if you stay on course, keeping your eye on the life-map and the God-signs as your father David did, I'll also give you a long life." (1 Kings 3:9-14)

Solomon wanted wisdom and knowledge. Is this true of us? If we polled graduating classes of America's best MBA programs, I wonder if "wisdom" or "knowledge" would be on the list of the top five things people want in life. You might hear:

- "I want to run my own business."
- "I want to be the CEO of a Fortune 500 company."
- "I want to be the pastor of a megachurch."

Asking for knowledge and wisdom set Solomon apart. He asked for a "God-listening heart." This is where knowledge begins. This is the birthplace of wisdom.

As leaders, the more we grow in our ability to listen to God, the more we also grow in our knowledge of our own finiteness, limited ability and vulnerability. We accept how much we do not know. We accept our limited abilities as leaders because we quickly learn and confess that "I cannot do everything well. I need others around me to make up for my inadequacies and limitations." We confess our vulnerability because we know that, by ourselves, we are weak no matter what others may think. We need others to complete what we cannot do alone. This kind of knowledge is true knowledge.

To ask for knowledge like Solomon did is really a confession of need. Every great leader is really a needy individual. Leaders who need others and lean into the wisdom of others are wise leaders. Leaders who develop the ability to listen to God and bow low in their leadership and defer to God are knowledgeable leaders. As leaders, we grow the ears of an elephant to listen for God's whispers. Yes, sometimes God whispers to us in the "still, small voice" that the prophet Elijah experienced. At other times, God seems to shout. As C. S. Lewis said, "God shouts to us in pain." Pain does in fact get our attention, doesn't it?

It's remarkable that in Luke's story of the transfiguration, we find God speaking directly to Peter, James and John. What he says to them is important: "This is my Son, whom I have chosen; listen to him" (Luke 9:35 NIV). Of all the things God could have said, of all the things he could have chosen to explain (Why is there suffering, disease and tragedy? Why do bad things happen to good people?), God says, "Listen to Jesus."

This is what every leader needs to know. We need to know how to listen to Jesus. To listen to God requires us to make space for listening. We live in a noisy world—one filled with voices telling us what to do, what to think and how to behave. Listening to God requires a commitment to turn down the volume of outer noise and to be quiet, to become centered and focused. To listen to God's voice requires unhurried time in that place where the psalmist says knowing is birthed: "Be still, and know that I am God" (Psalm 46:10 NIV). When we listen to God, we reflect. And to reflect is different than to react. Many of our reactions are due to the fact that we didn't take time to reflect first. We write an email we regret later. We drop a voicemail we wish we could delete. If we take time more often to reflect—to be still—then we can be assured that we have listened well and lived well out of what we've heard.

As we listen, we think. We meditate. We chew things over. In that important space, the mud clears. Deep, soulful impressions are made in the stillness. In the quiet, we become aware of what is right—we know what we must do and resolve to do it.[3]

Jonathan Edwards is widely regarded as one of the most important historical voices of American philosophy and theology. In the eighteenth century Edwards wrote these words:

> 'Tis one thing wherein man differs from the brute creatures, that he is cable of self-refection—of reflecting upon his own actions and what happens in his own mind and considering the nature and quality thereof, and doubtless it was partly for this end that God gave us this power that is denied other creatures, that we might know ourselves and consider our ways.[4]

Knowing ourselves. There is another aspect of knowledge that is essential for growth. We need to know ourselves—all of ourselves: our angels as well as our demons, our strengths as well as our limitations and weaknesses, our capabilities as well as the deep stuff that is often suppressed—desires, longings and fears.

John Calvin, one of the leading reformers of the church, wrote, "Nearly all wisdom we possess, that is to say, true and sound wisdom, consists of two parts: the knowledge of God and of ourselves." Along the journey in life, as we learn about God, we learn about ourselves.

We know that the human heart has four quadrants, which are all necessary to make the heart beat and move blood throughout the human body. I use this heart analogy to help leaders understand that in leadership, we must lead from all four quadrants, not just the top one. Let me explain.

The first quadrant of a heart-led leader is what you see on the surface. You hear the leader speak, but you may not see or know all the other factors that have shaped his decisions, philosophy or values. The second quadrant of a leader reveals more. You learn more from the leader by watching and listening to her. You hear her stories. You know some facts about her past. But you also realize how much you still don't know about the leader from the second quadrant. You know nothing of her past. You know little about her family. You know barely anything about what's inside the closet at home or the closets of the soul. Something may be hidden there—something important—but you're not invited into that quadrant yet.

The third quadrant of a leader's heart is reserved for a few of the leader's closet and most trusted friends. There's not room in the third quadrant for many people, because in this deep place we know people can fail us, forsake us and betray us. We let into our third quadrant only those we really trust and love—especially the dear friends that love us back, hopefully unconditionally.

The fourth quadrant is that place in a leader's heart that the leader himself or herself may not even know much about. Here addictions lurk like demons. Here—deep down, way down—lie motivations we're not really clear about, desires we have never explored, longings that may not be redeemed. By the way, it is into this quadrant that Jesus speaks so powerfully, telling us what really resides deep in a person's heart:

> It's what comes out of a person that pollutes: obscenities, lusts, thefts, murders, adulteries, greed, depravity, deceptive dealings, carousing, mean looks, slander, arrogance, foolishness—all these are vomit from the heart. *There* is the source of your pollution. (Mark 7:20-23)

Jesus is saying that the fourth quadrant of the heart is where we need to do the work within the work. If we do not bring light to what is deep within, we remain trapped in the dungeons of the fourth-quadrant heart. Left alone, the things Jesus mentions trip us up, make us fall, lure us into the cords that tie us up and leave us powerless—prisoners, not victors. Here, the Inside Job is essential. And listen to me clearly: no leader gets a free pass here. All of us are capable of living in the pollution of what we hold in the dark of the fourth quadrant.

A leader must descend through the four quadrants of his or her own heart to find that place where the dark things lie in wait. The unsuspecting leader wrongly assumes there are no inner demons, no dark forces that incubate jealousy, envy, unresolved anger and more.

Our résumé is not complete until our list of vital accomplishments shows a journey that has incorporated a thirst for knowing ourselves, our demons and our own story.[5] Above, I discussed having a God-listening heart, but leaders need to develop a people-listening heart as well. I've been amazed when working with leaders to realize how few actually try to listen to the folks they lead and who are perhaps subordinate to them. A good leader listens to the stories of others. People's stories contain all the information we need to connect the dots in our own minds as to why they do the things they do. It's all in their stories.

I listened this past week to a marketplace leader share a story of sexual abuse as a child. He seemed to quickly dismiss it as irrelevant to his current life and situation. But as he explored this incident, he saw the roots anchored deep in his heart that had affected his own sexual development and twisted his understanding of sexual gratification—an understanding that led him into years of a very unfortunate sexual addiction.

Every leader needs to look inside at the same time they are looking on the outside of the organization they are leading. It is there, deep inside, where motives lie, where hurts of the past reside. It is within ourselves that we find that moment when we made vows to ourselves and swallowed lies about ourselves that became fixed to our souls. Inside is where prejudice is birthed. It is where hatred is born. It is where unhealthy and unresolved feelings wait like dormant hungry bears who sleep through the snowy winters.

Deep within every human heart is the place where shame lies: Vocational shame, when we were fired or when we did something unethical that we now deeply regret. Sexual shame, when we acted differently from how we would act today. Emotional shame, when we believed the lies of parents, teachers and coaches who told us, "You'll never amount to anything." Educational shame, when we failed to study and grasp what was available to us and therefore live in ignorance now. In our culture today, many leaders suppress the shame they carry because there are so many other standards they feel compelled to meet—who can measure up when the bar is constantly being raised?

To know yourself requires time to reflect on your story—your history, your linear events of life, annotated with what was happening inside you as you moved along that timeline. Who were the primary shapers of your morals and values? Where were you living and how did those places affect you? My wife and I love the coastal islands and beaches of North Carolina—the place where we both grew up and our stories unfolded. This place helped make us who we are. We are all the places we have been, all the people we have touched and who have touched us, and all the relationships we have experienced. It's all packed within us and what is within us is our story. Do you know your story?

Within our stories, we discover what Brené Brown, author of *Daring Greatly* and *The Gift of Imperfection*, calls the "scarcity lie." It's the place within us where feelings of scarcity hold us in their grip:

- Never good enough.
- Never perfect enough.
- Never thin enough.
- Never powerful enough.
- Never successful enough.
- Never smart enough.
- Never certain enough.
- Never safe enough.
- Never extraordinary enough.[6]

We live with the haunting fear that we are not enough, and this fear cripples us and thwarts our desire to live a good life—a life that is satisfying and fulfilling. The good life we want is hijacked by feelings within that have never been examined but often been pressed down as we have busied ourselves with our outer life, attempting to add more markers of success to our list of merit badges. We compare our accomplishments with others and freeze in our efforts to keep up. Or we tap into what we think is our "high capacity" to lead better, pressing on and through walls instead of sitting down in their shadow to dismantle and understand them. We attempt to jump over these walls and catch our emotional Achilles heel on them—which has in fact been bothering us for years; we just didn't know what "it" was. What is the "it" that has been nagging you that needs to be examined right now? Who can help you look under the rocks along your path that might reveal interesting insights that have gone unseen and unnoticed for years?

All this knowledge helps us become a person of empathy—a person who shows understanding. Empathy is the transaction of seeking to identify with another person. A good leader identifies with her competitors as well as her clients; he identifies with the strong as well as the weak. True empathy is the seedbed where we live for each other and is the place where we choose to not be against each other. It is what Ralph Waldo Emerson describes in his phrase "the common heart." It is searching for that place inside of you that is shared by another. Writer and priest Henri Nouwen puts it this way:

> When we honestly ask ourselves which person in our lives means the most to us, we often find that it is those who, instead of giving advice, solutions, or cures, have chosen rather to share our pain and touch our wounds with a warm and tender hand. The friend who can be silent with us in a moment of despair or confusion, who can stay with us in an hour of grief and bereavement, who can tolerate not knowing, not curing, not healing and face with us the reality of our powerlessness, that is a friend who cares.[7]

I've experienced a lot of leaders who know the Bible quite well. They can quote verses and name all the books of the Bible but seem clueless about their own shortcomings and idiosyncrasies at work and in their relationships. Knowledge is more than amassing facts. It is submitting to the mystery that people are not mass-produced like widgets but are in fact "fearfully and wonderfully made," as the psalmist confesses in Psalm 139:14. When understood this way, knowledge opens us up to understand personalities, tendencies and quirks—our own as well as those of the people we live and work with. Knowledge says, "It's not just about me. I want to understand and value your perspective, your insights and your views." True knowledge bows in the presence of community and submits one's rights, authority and position to the power of the other.

Self-Control

At first we might think of self-control as managing our anger or not swearing when we're frustrated or startled. But as we look more deeply at our own hearts, we realize that self-control is about the practice of boundaries. Author and theologian Eugene Peterson has translated "self-control" in *The Message* as being "able to marshal and direct our energies wisely" (Galatians 5:23). Self-control in leadership is less about managing sins and more about understanding our margin—the space between ourselves and our limits, our capacity, what we can accomplish without leaving ourselves depleted. Leaders who give must also be given to, and this is especially true with energy—when we give it out we must also take it in.

We marshal our energy wisely so our life is not controlled by someone else, so that we are not taken advantage of, so that we are not "used." Healthy boundaries exist to help us be responsible, to act in healthy ways toward others, and to keep us from running our lives on empty. Let's explore three areas where today's leaders need to practice self-control: energy, relational bandwidth and capacity to care.

Energy. Physical, emotional and spiritual energy must be replenished regularly. These are not inexhaustible resources. A leader needs to recognize and exercise self-control in how much energy he or she gives out each day, each week, each month and each year. When we do not regulate the flow out as well as the flow in, we end up burned out, exhausted and spent.

Sherry is the mother of three preschoolers, the wife of a busy leader, and a part-time employee at a local bank. She gives her all in each role she finds herself in at any moment, with little left for herself. Sherry told me, "Sometimes I feel like I'm nothing more than a gas pump—always filling everyone else up." We spent some time exploring ways Sherry could find her own way to be filled each week so that she would not run her life on empty. Exploring how to be "filled" is not a selfish act. It is an exercise in self-control. To live life feeling thin and tired all the time is to have no boundaries for yourself, to have no self-control. We end up becoming gluttons for punishment—in other words, victims.

I can remember in my younger years going on business trips and working every possible minute on my flight to the next location. I had swallowed the lie along with so many others: If I'm busy, then I'm important. Now I see more clearly. Today I rarely work on an airplane. My general rule for travel is to sleep and replenish whenever I can. If I can't sleep, I read a novel. My subrule is not to read anything overly taxing. A good spy thriller or adventure story serves me well—pure non-intellectual entertainment. This helps me recharge my battery.

Relational capacity. Our relational capacity is our ability to maintain healthy relationships, and leaders need to practice self-control in interactions with other people no matter how extroverted or people-oriented they think they are. Relationships are necessary and vital for us to live at our best, but not all people are life-giving. Exercising self-control means to be aware of those people who give life and those who drain it. Who makes you laugh until it hurts? Who challenges you and inspires you to become a better version of yourself? These are the people we want and need to be around. But who drains you? Who takes and takes and takes when you give and give and give? This kind of relationship is not reciprocal. We need to be careful here, and we need to be wise. Some people have the ability to steal grace from us.

Gwen loves for me to spend time with my friend Rick. She hears me laugh until I cry at his jokes and mannerisms. When I spend time with Rick I feel rejuvenated. So in my schedule, I try to spend regular time with people like Rick. They are investments in my well-being. They care. They love me well and they want my best. Other people do not seek out my well-being. They need me to listen, to care, to be emotionally and spiritually invested in them. For me, that is work, not leisure. That is something I do when I'm on the clock, so to speak. As I monitor my relational capacity, I realize I need life-giving friends on a consistent basis.

It's interesting to me to remember that the apostle Peter had two close associates with whom he traveled and interacted during his journey with Jesus. The Gospels repeatedly tell us of this microgroup within the twelve disciples: Peter, James and John. I think that this microgroup offered Jesus—even Jesus—something that the larger group, including Thomas the doubter, Judas the betrayer and others, simply could not.

Capacity to care. People who give are subject to what is called "compassion fatigue." Without proper monitoring and self-care, we can simply grow weary of caring, which causes us to become cynical, sarcastic and hardened. I see this all the time in my work with leaders. Cynicism and sarcasm are real indicators of the thinness of someone's soul. We usually become cynical and sarcastic when we are exhausted and feel down about something or someone.

If we find that we hurt when we care, a yellow flashing warning light needs to go off in our soul. This hurt is different from compassion—compassion allows us to enter someone else's pain without it entering our own soul. To care well means to marshal our energy and our passion and to maintain a boundary between the one who is in pain and the one who brings comfort and healing. Can a caregiver cry upon hearing a heart-wrenching story? Of course. I do all the time. But if my tears flow for myself rather than the one I am caring for, I have crossed a line. Some distance gives the caregiver much-needed perspective. The one who is caring well maintains a sort of three-dimensional perspective, and he or she is able to rise up and see the larger picture of what may be happening beyond just the pain of the moment.

A caring leader came to me after working for a long time in a country that has many needs and problems. He started the conversation this way: "I'm here, but I feel like I'm in a coma. I'm numb. I feel indifferent to everyone and everything—including God. I don't even want to care anymore. I can't care anymore. I don't have care in me. It's gone!"

Through our time together we explored this deadness of heart, the annihilation that had come about through this leader's attempts to be savior to everyone. As he spent time alone he explored some of the mistakes he had made in not practicing self-care, or "soul care," as I call it. Then I saw him slowly come back to life. He spent time in God's creation, in quiet, in prayer and in conversation with me. All this time helped revive him, if not resurrect him right before my eyes. What was happening was a "trickle charge." A leader learns to trickle-charge by allowing time, a place apart and solitude to do what no other power on earth can do. We receive a slow infusion of life back into our depleted bodies and spent souls.

We can't speed up a trickle charge. When my car battery goes dead, I can go get my jumper cables and hook up another car's batteries and jump-start my dead car. But as leaders we cannot be jump-started when we're depleted inside. It won't work. We have to do what Jesus did: pull away and detach from others and simply begin to trickle-charge back to life.

I once read a book in which the author said everyone needed a private relaxation activity—something that was a "no-brainer." For a friend of his, it was raking leaves in the driveway. For the author, it was ironing his shirts. For my friend Brian, a CEO of a gas company, it is (believe it or not) washing dishes—much to the joy of his wife Nan and their kids! Brian told me that his daughter Brie sometimes says, "Dad, you look stressed so I am leaving my dishes in the sink for you to wash." Isn't that thoughtful?

This is perhaps the most common misunderstanding I see in companies, organizations and churches today. Those who give must also receive! A leader cannot keep giving and giving. No one can give 110 percent day after day. It's just not possible. No one is the Energizer bunny we see in the ads—that wound-up rabbit that keeps moving, keeps trudging no matter what. That was not one of the ways of Jesus. We're told by the medical doctor Luke, who witnessed the lifestyle and ways of Jesus, that "Jesus often withdrew to lonely places" (Luke 5:16 NIV). Here's the secret: Something happens in a lonely place that does not, cannot and will not happen in a board room, conference center, sanctuary or coliseum. A leader must be about the Inside Job of discovering and experiencing what that "something" is—and do it.

Caring can lead to depletion. Depletion can lead to depression. Depression is a root of burnout, and when you are burned out you care for no one, including yourself. Understanding and knowing your limits helps you to avoid burning out and running your life on empty. It's your Inside Job to know what your limits are and to honor them. If you stretch a rubber band beyond its own ability to stretch, it will snap. Let me be clear. Stretching is good. But it is not good to be stretched beyond what is actually possible.

A Nobel Prize–winning model. Mother Teresa, the Nobel Prize–winning nun, marshaled the energy of the Brothers and Sisters of Charity wisely. She realized that as these caregivers ministered compassionately to the sick and dying in Calcutta, India, they could not face that kind of dire need seven days a week. So she set up a schedule:

- Work in the wake of need for six days. But you must be away from need on the seventh day. Everyone has a Sabbath—a day to cease every six days.

- Work in that rhythm for three weeks. But on the fourth week, you are required to be away from need, helping the dying, and giving comfort to the ill for an entire week.

- Work in that rhythm for eleven months and you must be out and away from helping people for an entire month.

- Work in that rhythm for several years, then take an extended time—a "sabbatical"—for an entire year.

This sustainable rhythm—this self-control—allowed people to live, serve and work without burnout. They could work hard, because they knew that their week, their month or their entire year's worth of break was right around the corner.

In my work with hundreds of leaders, I find that this concept is extremely difficult and even offensive to some. One CEO told me, "Mother Teresa must have had a lazy bone in her. I can't afford to do that, Steve." But we discover as we work long and hard that there simply must be a model of living and working that can sustain us.

I believe the Mother Teresa rhythm is one of the great models for leadership today. When we feel indispensible and assume that we cannot back off, take off or embrace a sustainable rhythm, we are taking ourselves far too seriously. Self-control is a virtue because when we live with self-control and practice self-control, we actually practice a great truth. The greater truth is this. God is in control. I am not. God is big. I am small. God embraces a 24/7 rhythm for us. I am not God. I am not the savior.

As the world turns. In our busy, demanding world, self-control is one of the greatest virtues we need to develop. The tyranny of the urgent and the nonstop pace of our lives gnaw at the very platform upon which we are living our lives and trying to help others, whether in business or ministry. In my work with leaders, this is the single, most violated virtue I consistently see in the soul at work. When I point it out, most leaders initially play the victim role. They confess their powerlessness. They feel like there is nothing they can do about their schedule. But this is not the truth. And when we don't embrace the truth, we live in a lie. It's a lie to resign yourself to powerlessness.

To grow in self-control requires us to examine our motivations for doing the work we do. For me, I realized that not all my motives were pure in my work as a caregiver, a senior leader of a mega-church, and the leader of a nonprofit organization. I wanted to be liked, loved and celebrated, and I learned that the church world would always applaud my workaholism. I don't recall an elder, deacon or peer ever stopping me and making me examine why I was working so hard. It wasn't until I hit a wall in my late thirties that I began to examine the darker side of my leadership. I began the journey then of doing my own Inside Job. Until I hit the wall, I never knew there really was an Inside Job that needed my attention. I just worked, and I worked a lot. It was only through doing the work within my own work—the very same work that I'm asking you to do here—that I realized the abuse I was subjecting myself to, the abuse I was exposing my wife to, and the loss I was experiencing despite what appeared to be gain. In this season it hit me: I had given the best years of my life to my work. My wife and my children? They got the leftovers of my time, energy and passion.

I began a long season of recovery. I have shared this story extensively in *The Lazarus Life*, where I compare my self to Lazarus who died and was buried.[8] Jesus finally came to raise his friend Lazarus, but as Lazarus came out of the tomb, he appeared in all of his grave clothes. And we have to get rid of the old grave clothes if we really want to live. I did and so will you!

There is a better way to live than this crazy way we are living. And it is our work within the work to find this way and live in it.

6

The Great Eight Virtues, Part Two

*Perseverance, Godliness,
Kindness and Love*

Peter knew what leadership requires from two perspectives. First, he was a small business owner. As a marketplace leader in his own day, Peter knew that character mattered. Second, his vocation changed when he began to follow Jesus. And his description of the interior work leaders must do flows from this perspective. They must persevere and not quit. They must emulate the God they follow in their actions. They are to choose kindness as a primary descriptor of their leadership ethos. Above all, leaders are to lead with love, not with the authority that comes from an office, title or position. Let's look at the second half of Peter's list of eight virtues from 2 Peter 1.

Perseverance

In our throwaway culture, if something doesn't work, we just throw it away and get a new one—new microwave, new car, new chair, new can opener. In fact, certain marketing agents realize that many people actually prefer to get a new gadget rather than fix a broken one, simply because we don't have time or the skill to fix it. We've lost our perspective on endurance and persevering through a difficult season.

In my career I have been a senior church leader, pioneered and founded two churches, and founded a nonprofit organization that requires me to raise my own salary and benefits—something I continue to do to this day. The nonprofit purchased a thirty-five–acre ranch with money I had raised, and the national economy tanked within months of our closing. This real estate deal could easily have morphed into a nightmare. Let me be honest: it has taken nothing but sheer unadulterated perseverance for me to be able to survive and learn how to foster a sense of thriving.

Pioneering a new business, planting a new church or starting anything new is an invitation for difficulties, failure and opposition. It's been a long, long journey, most of it uphill. To give up and do something easier has, of course, crossed my mind—mostly when I'm in a downcast season of life. I often find that when I am tired, alone and discouraged, this is the perfect storm of realities to make me want to quit and give up.

Several years ago the movie *The Perfect Storm* told the story of a group of fishermen who invested their lives catching fish off the coast of New England. One season, three different storms converged, morphing into a perfect storm of such epic proportions that it simply could not be survived under any circumstances. We all have storms brewing—things that with only a little more intensity could become major tempests in our lives. Be on the lookout for your own "perfect storm" that can cause you to want to give up and quit.

The way to struggle well against the desire to give up is to engage in three responses to the perfect storm's components. When you're tired, make sure you rest and rest well. When you are alone, let this be a flashing light that you need community to share the load. And finally, when you are discouraged, this is the call to tend to the weary soul and body. The literal meaning of "discouragement" says it all: to deprive the heart of courage. I believe the best response is to have people "speak into you"—to listen to the voices of those you respect and who matter to you. Grow Velcro in your heart and allow their words to stick to you—in you and to your soul.

Political activist and former president of South Africa Nelson Mandela has become a legend to us in perseverance and endurance. He was imprisoned for twenty-seven years, but his prison cell became a birthplace for endurance, not a cesspool of bitterness. He has written the following:

> I have walked that long road to freedom. I have tried not to falter; I have made missteps along the way. But I have discovered the secret that after climbing a great hill, one only finds that there are many more hills to climb. I have taken a moment here to rest, to steal a view of the glorious vista that surrounds me, to look back on the distance I have come. But I can only rest for a moment, for with freedom come responsibilities, and I dare not linger, for my long walk is not ended.[1]

Mandela wrote this after serving years in prison, leading hundreds of demonstrations and talking to thousands of leaders about his vision for freedom for the black South Africans who were being unjustly treated and inhumanely regarded. What would have happened if Nelson Mandela had not persevered? What if he had given up?

I ask this same question about other leaders who led in austere and challenging times. I look not through the lens of a political party but I look into the lens of the hearts of such women and men. Perseverance requires heart—a courageous heart, a heart filled with hope and sheer determination to stand at a closed door and wait. It may be an issue of timing and nothing else as to when the door will open a crack—a crack that is an invitation to walk through.

Perseverance, though, requires more than heart. It requires setting your face like flint to move forward in the direction you know you have to go. The expression "set his face like flint" comes from a description of Jesus when it was time for him to go to Jerusalem, where he knew he would be killed (see Luke 9:51).[2] He "set his face like flint" and went no place else but Jerusalem. That is perseverance. That is a resolve to go forward when everything else is pushing you back.

The words of C. S. Lewis are helpful to us here: "Never, in peace or war, commit your virtue or your happiness to the future. Happy work is best done by the man who takes his long-term plans somewhat lightly and works from moment to moment 'as to the Lord.' It is only our daily bread that we are encouraged to ask for. The present is the only time in which any duty can be done or any grace received."[3] Our duty is to persevere. What makes Lewis's words so poignant and powerful is that he delivered them in a sermon to soldiers facing the Normandy invasion of 1945—men and women who would surely persevere through pain and agony for a cause that impassioned their hearts to press on, to press forward—even unto death.

Godliness

The word "godliness" is simply not in the lexicon of many people I encounter these days. I don't find many people using the word, much less understanding what it means. So let me explain it in a way that will help us not only to desire to be godly but motivate us to embrace this ancient word, virtue and quality.

Godliness is the mark of someone's life when she espouses the virtues listed by Peter. When a person lives with virtues and by virtues, his life is characterized more by heaven's values than by the world's. Godliness is the quality of life that shows reverence for God and for the things of God. While this word is rarely used today, it is a virtue that followers of Jesus are encouraged to attain. Later on Peter says, "You ought to live holy and godly lives" (2 Peter 3:11 NIV). Godliness is the quality of a person's life that is like God's own heart and life. To be godly is to be like God.

In our competitive, busy and fast-paced life, we are prone to forget what our real goal is. We may want to be successful, but do we want to be godly? The apostle Paul reminds us that being like Jesus is our ultimate goal, not being successful or being wealthy. We are to be like Jesus (2 Corinthians 3:18; Romans 8:29; Galatians 4:19). This is the line of demarcation that differentiates the life of a follower of Jesus and the life of any other person who follows anything at all—to follow Jesus is to be on the path of becoming like him.

When my friend Scott became a follower of Jesus in his university days, his life began to change immediately. He gave up drinking to get drunk, dating women to have sex, and cheating his way through his studies to get better grades. As he studied the life of Jesus, he realized that his behavior needed to be adjusted. He began to "clean up his life," as he put it. He learned new ways of living that brought a deeper sense of contentment, happiness and peace than he had ever experienced before. His outer markers of success began to change and he set his focus on the inner markers that we are discussing here. When Scott opened his medical engineering business, he made a commitment to give some of the profits to organizations he believed in. As his business grew, so did his share of giving—and so did his godliness.

The work of being godly is a slow, steady work at the deepest level of our lives. It is what author Eugene Peterson calls a "long obedience in the same direction."[4] To set our goal to become a godly person is to expose all of our life to the high bar of God's standards and ways. This quest will affect our health and lifestyle. It will affect our emotional life and will search for the peace of our past issues and hurts. It will affect how we treat the people we live and work with. To set one's goal to be godly is to open one's heart, all four quadrants, even the darkest secrets never before exposed to anyone. Paul tells one of his students, Titus, "We're being shown how to turn our backs on a godless, indulgent life, and how to take on a God-filled, God-honoring life" (Titus 2:11-13). A God-honoring life. That is what it means to be godly.

Pursuing godliness means even our desires will be transformed. Sometimes I crave a good ol' "Double Stuf" Oreo—perhaps a handful of them. But when going to the cabinet to sneak a few, I have to stop and ask myself this critical question: What do I want more than an Oreo? This question of desire forces me to get in the face of what I want, what I long for and what I think I need. What do I want more than an Oreo? I want my health. I want to lose the pounds I've gained over Christmas. I want to feel good. When my desire is changed to want the things of God, then I find myself well on the way to becoming the kind of person I really want to be. I find that I am actually becoming a better version of my true self—a version that really desires to live a God-honoring life, a God-devoted life, a God-loving life.

Brotherly Kindness

We are living in the days when children are bullied. People take advantage of others who are less fortunate. This has been called an age of violence. A popular new game in cities is called "Knockout," where innocent people are struck in the face as they innocently walk down a sidewalk. It's an age of road rage. It's an age of war. And in the midst of it all, we are called to be kind to one another.

In the midst of such times, we are called to exhibit a quality that is so stunning, so remarkable and so rare that it often stops us in our tracks—it's such a novelty that we'll sit and watch YouTube videos depicting acts of kindness. When Peter finally gets to brotherly kindness and love, we might think these virtues seem soft, irrelevant and even feminine. But as we explore them, let's find out how radical and necessary they are in our lives.

Peter reminds us earlier in his first epistle that we have "tasted the kindness of the Lord" (1 Peter 2:3 NASB). It is through kindness that something truly beyond ourselves enters into our life. Kindness is the lens through which we see the sacred. It's not about simply choosing to be kind for kindness's sake. It is about participating in a way of life that sees people as having worth and dignity, and in whom we see reflections of God. We often forget this simple truth in our dog-eat-dog world. Jesus' story of the Good Samaritan reveals the power of kindness. In the parable, Jesus tells us that those who by profession and reputation were supposed to be kind were actually bankrupt in this most basic virtue. But an outsider, a Samaritan who was despised and rejected because of his ethnicity, made a simple, kind gesture of caring for someone in need, and that one man now has a legacy known to millions of people down through the ages (see Luke 10:25-37). Simple acts of kindness reveal a sacred force behind the act. The well-known preacher and author Frederick Buechner writes, "Be kind because although kindness is not by a long shot the same thing as holiness, kindness is one of the doors that holiness enters the world through, enters us through—not just gently kind but sometimes fiercely kind."[5]

It's not rocket science. A veterinarian closes his office for a short time each day. On the door a note is posted that says, "We're closed every day from 12:00 to 2 p.m. for the benefit of our employees so that they can run errands and come back fully committed to helping your pet get well and stay well." A megachurch rings a bell at ten a.m. and again at two-thirty p.m. for all staff to come out of their offices and cubicles and meet in a gathering area for tea and coffee. A small staff decides not to text, email or call each other on their days off so they can truly be "off" and not be reminded of work details until they return.

It's really not hard to be kind. But it does take courage to be different and treat others well. What's at stake is how we view each other. Kindness is based on seeing God in another person's face when you're tempted to ignore, be mean or say something harsh. An old quote attributed to Philo of Alexandria says, "Be kind, for everyone is involved in a great battle." How true this is. When we recognize that life is difficult and we have no idea what others are facing in their private world, why not exercise kindness? Doesn't it stand to reason that our capacity for kindness is proportional to our understanding of the common battle we face as humans?

Love

Peter is not alone in showing us a progressive list of virtues that people should possess. Paul does it also (see Romans 12:9-21; Colossians 3:12-14). But no matter what list we read and who wrote it, love is always the highest-ranked quality. Paul uses the analogy of virtues being put on like clothes. He ends his wardrobe requirement for leaders this way: "Regardless of what else you put on, wear love. It's your basic, all-purpose garment. Never be without it" (Colossians 3:14).

Here's the truth of today's world: we have forgotten love. Oh sure, we use the word in our private lives, but what of our corporate ways? Is there no place for what matters most in our work? We are to love one another, period. It's impossible for us to read the words of Jesus and other New Testament writers without realizing how many times we are told to love each other. Yet how devoid of love so many of us are. There are seminars and webinars to help us be better leaders, better managers, better salespeople. But what about being better at love?

It's interesting how elementary an approach Paul and Peter take with those in their movement—the movement of following Jesus. They assume little and teach them the most basic forms of what it means to do almost everything: how to pray, how to regard the Scriptures, how to treat a spouse and much more. When it comes to love, Paul places the cookies on the lowest shelf possible so no one misses out on the meaning or the implication. Remember, the people these apostles addressed were not seasoned veterans in following Jesus. They were newbies, perhaps involved in other movements that ran counter to the movement of God through the life and teachings of Jesus. What they needed to know was that nothing on this earth replaces the power of love. Nothing.

I want to include here one of the most amazing chapters in the entire Bible, one that is read at many weddings and other occasions but is appropriate to examine here in full. It's Paul's description of love found in 1 Corinthians 13. Read it slowly, allowing the words to penetrate your mind and heart:

> If I speak with human eloquence and angelic ecstasy but don't love, I'm nothing but the creaking of a rusty gate.
>
> If I speak God's Word with power, revealing all his mysteries and making everything plain as day, and if I have faith that says to a mountain, "Jump," and it jumps, but I don't love, I'm nothing.
>
> If I give everything I own to the poor and even go to the stake to be burned as a martyr, but I don't love, I've gotten nowhere. So, no matter what I say, what I believe, and what I do, I'm bankrupt without love.
>
> Love never gives up.
> Love cares more for others than for self.
> Love doesn't want what it doesn't have.
> Love doesn't strut,
> Doesn't have a swelled head,

Doesn't force itself on others,
Isn't always "me first,"
Doesn't fly off the handle,
Doesn't keep score of the sins of others,
Doesn't revel when others grovel,
Takes pleasure in the flowering of truth,
Puts up with anything,
Trusts God always,
Always looks for the best,
Never looks back,
But keeps going to the end.

Love never dies. Inspired speech will be over some day; praying in tongues will end; understanding will reach its limit. We know only a portion of the truth, and what we say about God is always incomplete. But when the Complete arrives, our incompletes will be canceled.

When I was an infant at my mother's breast, I gurgled and cooed like any infant. When I grew up, I left those infant ways for good.

We don't yet see things clearly. We're squinting in a fog, peering through a mist. But it won't be long before the weather clears and the sun shines bright! We'll see it all then, see it all as clearly as God sees us, knowing him directly just as he knows us!

But for right now, until that completeness, we have three things to do to lead us toward that consummation: Trust steadily in God, hope unswervingly, love extravagantly. And the best of the three is love. (1 Corinthians 13:1-13)

It's very clear, Paul says: "We have three things to do to lead us toward that consummation: Trust steadily in God, hope unswervingly, love extravagantly." And to underscore it all, he trumps that with a final word: "The best of the three is love."

Let me ask you a question. What if this chapter were read in board meetings, staff meetings and leadership gatherings? What if we, like both Paul and Peter, assumed we needed to aim for the simple in our team settings and said, "Folks, we're going to begin our meeting with one of the famous and often-quoted pieces of literature in the world and it's on love. Ready? Here it is." And you then read this ethical magna carta on what is required of us to get along with each other.

Team conflict is the number one reason missionaries are fired from their jobs and sent home. Conflict among staff members everywhere is an everyday occurrence. Ninety percent of all partnerships fail because of a falling out between partners. More than half of all marriages fail here—and the statistics go on. The truth is this: We simply do not know how to love each other well. There is a better way to relate. A prayer by the monk and author Thomas Merton echoes our plea:

> Give me the strength that waits upon you in silence and peace. Give me humility in which alone is rest, and deliver me from pride which is the heaviest of burdens. Possess my whole heart and soul with the simplicity of love. Occupy my whole life with the one thought and the one desire of love, that I may love not for the sake of merit, not for the sake of perfection, not for the sake of virtue, not for the sake of sanctity, but for You alone.[6]

The four postures of loving well. There are four postures we need to assume when we seek to implement the virtue of love. While there are myriad books on this subject (some of which I recommend in the workbook), let me explain here four ways to love well.

First, listen well. To listen is to love. Listening is not about stating our opinion, offering our perspective or asserting our birth order.

Loving well means listening deeply to the other person. Counselors and addiction therapists Dale and Juanita Ryan tell us:

> It is a remarkable experience to have someone really listen— to have someone's undivided attention and interest. When someone listens, they communicate to us on a very deep level that we are valuable. Their listening breaks our isolation and aloneness. And it decreases the fears which come when our thoughts and feelings are confused. Talking out loud in the presence of a person who listens carefully allows us to gain clarity and perspective. Gradually, being listened to can begin to convince us that we are worth someone's attention and worth being loved. When someone listens with respect and acceptance we are comforted and consoled. Our pain is soothed. Our burden is lightened.[7]

Second, be willing to be hurt. Love requires both the person seeking to love and the one receiving love to be mindful of the probability of pain. C. S. Lewis has written a wonderful book for those of us who want to understand love better. He writes:

> To love at all is to be vulnerable. Love anything and your heart will be wrung and possibly broken. If you want to make sure of keeping it intact you must give it to no one, not even an animal. Wrap it carefully round with hobbies and little luxuries; avoid all entanglements. Lock it up safe in the casket or coffin of your selfishness. But in that casket, safe, dark, motionless, airless, it will change. It will not be broken; it will become unbreakable, impenetrable, irredeemable. To love is to be vulnerable.[8]

Third, value the one you are seeking to love well. Treat the other person with respect, dignity and honor. Respect his views and opinions. Invite her perspective. Show him you are interested. Be careful here, as many people can smell a rat in this domain. If people feel manipulated by a sudden interest when they have been treated like a doormat up to this point, then you have more work of restoration to do.

Finally, to love well means that we bless the other person. We don't have to agree, but we do need to bless. To bless someone is to speak words of affirmation, healing and encouragement. To bless is to courageously tell someone you wish her well, that you want God's best for him, that you appreciate her and what she has done. This does not mean we beg the person to stay or coerce him or her to do what we feel is right. To bless is also to release the other person to the next place, the next team or the next organization with the hope that it will go well there—even though it may not have gone well with us. Love must be expressed. Unexpressed love makes love benign rather than powerful and effective. When we share how we feel, how much we value our colleague or team member or spouse, this ignites something reciprocal. Taking this posture of love breeds loyalty. It fosters care. It creates love.

You may be thinking, "Steve, this is the real world. We don't bless people in corporate America!" To that I simply say, "Why not?" Try to bless the people around you and see if you can observe a difference in their attitude or their behavior. Even if things get hard and someone leaves your company or staff, try to bless that person. Words have the power to bridge gaps and heal hearts. When properly spoken, words of blessing affirm the heart and validate what is most true about the one receiving the blessing.

You'd think the church would have this down. But sadly, in my work with leaders in the church, I find that many of them walk around empty inside because no one ever really spoke into their hearts and thanked them for their presence and service. Sad but true. To bless is to breathe life. To not bless is to withhold life.

Henri Nouwen reminds us that "a blessing goes beyond the distinction between admiration or condemnation, between virtues or vices, between good deed or evil deeds. A blessing touches the original goodness of the other and calls forth his or her Belovedness."[9] A blessing can be more valuable than an engraved watch or coupon for a dinner out. Only words have the power to build us up from the inside out.

While it may seem like we're talking about different topics in the next three chapters—things like rhythm and limits and transitions—the truth is that these flow directly from the eight virtues we've just covered. Without the foundation of the eight virtues, these three very important areas in a leader's life are guaranteed to implode. This may happen later rather than sooner, but rest assured, it will happen.

7

THE LEADER'S RHYTHM

Exposing the Lie of Being Balanced

◆◆◆

Rhythm is God's way of helping us live resilient lives. When first understood, then practiced, rhythm is transformational in not only how to live but how to thrive. It is truly revolutionary in the way we learn to look at and experience life.

In 1509 Nicolas Copernicus revolutionized the world and established a new reality of understanding when he unveiled his theory that the sun, not the earth, was the center of the universe. Everything began to change with this new way of looking at life. Rhythm can have the same power to completely change the way you live. Copernicus did not invent the new heliocentric universe. He simply stated what had always been true but people had failed to realize.

Rhythm is not my invention—far from it. It is as old as creation. We are told from the very beginning of time that God set the world up in a foundational rhythm—a rhythm that continues to this very day. Here's how it is put for us:

Earth was a soup of nothingness, a bottomless emptiness, an inky blackness. God's Spirit brooded like a bird above the watery abyss.

God spoke: "Light!"
    And light appeared.
God saw that light was good
    and separated light from dark.
God named the light Day,
    he named the dark Night.
It was evening, it was morning—
Day One. (Genesis 1:1-5)

God created from nothingness a span of time called a "day"—a period of time when the light of the sun Copernicus studied would beam its business to our small, fragile planet, and this light would mark the day while darkness would mark the night.

God spoke: "Lights! Come out!
    Shine in Heaven's sky!
Separate Day from Night.
    Mark seasons and days and years,
Lights in Heaven's sky to give light to Earth."
    And there it was. (Genesis 1:14-15)

Time is etched in an indelible rhythm of days, seasons and years. This rhythm is also engraved in every human soul that has ever lived. Calendars and human bodies, plants and beasts all function according to a basic rhythm: daily, weekly, monthly, quarterly and annually.

The human body functions according to a circadian rhythm. *Circa* is Latin for "around" and *diem* means "day." Doctors know very well that the human body is naturally set to a circadian rhythm. That's why some medicine is best taken at night, when your body will be at rest, and why other medicines are prescribed to be taken in the morning. This built-in rhythm is not designed by humans but by the Creator of the universe and everything in it.

We live by this rhythm every day. We get up in the morning and sleep at night if our work doesn't interfere with this natural rhythm. Jobs that require a shift in the rhythm will most likely pay an incentive to those willing to disrupt their lives and work according to a different pattern. We plan meetings, count on our vacations, take days off and more by this rhythm. It's inescapable.

Thousands of years after the Genesis account, a Hebrew poet sought to give expression to this rhythm of life in one of the Psalms. We find there these words that underscore a foundation of how life works:

> The moon keeps track of the seasons,
>   the sun is in charge of each day.
> When it's dark and night takes over,
>   all the forest creatures come out.
> The young lions roar for their prey,
>   clamoring to God for their supper.
> When the sun comes up, they vanish,
>   lazily stretched out in their dens.
> Meanwhile, men and women go out to work,
>   busy at their jobs until evening. (Psalm 104:19-23)

But wait just a moment. Go back and reread the very last line. It says, "Men and women go out to work, busy at their jobs until evening." That's the rhythm established by God and lived out for centuries: busy at their jobs *until evening*. And we have violated it.

Our violation of God's intended rhythm of life has thrown us out of sync. Feeling out of sync, we've resorted to trying to balance our lives. Balance is all the rage among busy people. "I want more balance in my life." "I feel out of balance." "I'm not balancing all the demands of my life well." We become like the man in the circus who spins plates on tiny rods. We run from one thing to the next, trying to keep the plates spinning but in fact seeing many of them crash and break around our feet. We feel out of control. We say we are running on empty. We lament that there must be a better way to live. And then we ask the sad question: Is this as good as it gets?

Dishonoring this rhythm results in something deeply wrong within us. Not only are we out of balance, but in the words of Thomas Merton, we are in a situation far, far more serious. He says it best: "To allow oneself to be carried away by a multitude of conflicting concerns, to surrender to too many demands, to commit oneself to too many projects, to want to help everyone in everything is so succumb to violence."[1] Violence. A violence within.

In my work with leaders in the marketplace and ministry, I've found that hardly anyone tells the truth when I ask—hopefully in front of their spouse—"How many hours a week do you think you work?" The answer is always shy of the reality. When I ask, "Do you check email and voicemail at night, after work?" Sheepishly nearly one hundred percent say, "Well, yes. Yes, I do." And here we find a big reason for why they have come to see me in the first place. So much being "on" makes you feel off.

Though we live in a 24/7 world, we were never created to function in one. We were created to work in one span of time and be off and rest in another. But who does that anymore? We constantly complain about being tired when we never really rest as intended by God who seeks to give to us even in our sleep! Another Hebrew poem points this out:

> It's useless to rise early and go to bed late,
> > and work your worried fingers to the bone.
> Don't you know he enjoys
> > giving rest to those he loves? (Psalm 127:2)

Today's work ethos is: "Be constantly available. Because if you don't, both you and your product will be replaced by your competitor who is lying in wait like a hungry African lion, ready to devour everything around him and then look for more after he licks his lips and rests awhile." This is not about being constantly available. This is about being constantly afraid.

Moving in Rhythm

When we talk about embracing rhythm, we are talking about modifying our behavior. Living in rhythm is about what we do and don't do. Whether or not we choose to rest, whether we decide to practice a Sabbath, whether we choose to turn off our phone and not look at email after we come home from a long day at work—all of these things are about our behavior. These things are also about choice. We can choose to live in a sustainable rhythm; we can choose to do something positive about our life. The question is, will we?

My wife and I operate a retreat house for leaders—Potter's Inn. It is located an hour's drive from the city. It sits on the shoulders of Pike's Peak, a mountain that is 14,132 feet high. In the winter, we see no bears. They hibernate. When the snow falls heavy in February and March, we see and hear no hummingbirds. They have taken off for their annual migration to Mexico where the air is warmer and the flowers bloom in all their glory. We have no bluebirds until April; they are in New Mexico and Arizona. Every living thing knows this rhythm—every living thing, it seems, except for human beings.

We modern and wired people thumb our nose at such ancient insight. We moderns have carved a new way of living that has no rhythm at all. It's exactly like the Hebrew prophet Jeremiah lamented:

Cranes know when it's time
    to move south for winter.
And robins, warblers, and bluebirds
    know when it's time to come back again.
But my people? My people know nothing,
    not the first thing of GOD and his rule. (Jeremiah 8:7)

Jeremiah lamented the condition of his time. Perhaps we need to lament ours. But that would be a waste of time, wouldn't it? Let's press on! Let's git 'er done. We hurry everyone up to live in a breathless condition that was never intended and is, in fact, a result of our own bent ways of perceiving reality—ways that are absolutely broken. After living in such a breathless way, we then seek balance. But as everyone knows who has tried to achieve balance, it simply does not work. When we try to live a balanced life, we end up managing categories or constantly reshaping pie slices of how we've envisioned our life. The word "balance" is not in any Bible we will ever read. But the concept of rhythm is not only in the Bible; it was lived by Jesus and modeled by the early church. The monastics revived a life of rhythm by insisting that church spires have bells in them that would ring at regular and predictable times of the day—calling people to pray. Rhythm offers a kinder, more gentle way to live.

Shalom

By embracing rhythm rather than balance, we engage in a doable, practiced and proven method that fosters resilience in life. Now, there's not a cookie cutter program for living in rhythm, for that would be more law—something none of us needs. But we do need to experience the unforced grace of renewal that is ours when we live in rhythm. One's outer rhythm fosters an inner cadence. By living in a well-defined rhythm of life, we redefine an inner life of order, rest and anticipation—all good things that help us find a much greater goal than productivity.

Inner rest is closely associated with an old Hebrew greeting— "Shalom!"—which we often wrongly translate as "peace." Its meaning is far, far deeper. Shalom is to live with well-being in mind, a well-being we wish for ourselves and others. And there is no well-being without rhythm. The goal of life is not to simply endure to the end. The hope of life is to enjoy life—and one of the greatest secrets is now out! When you live in rhythm you foster a life that is more about thriving than surviving, more about enjoying than enduring and more about joy than despair.

Shalom y'all!

Building a New Foundation

The handyman at our retreat center is building a new storage barn for us. One day as Charles and I were talking, he said, "The first and most important thing to do is to build a strong foundation. Because if we don't, the high winds could blow this thing right off the mountain." At our retreat center we sometimes have hurricane-force winds of over eighty miles per hour that whip around mountains and chase the valley floor, making it hard to even walk. A foundation is an essential part of building a new platform for how we want to live and embrace a life of rhythm.

When God first envisioned life, he envisioned it in a six-one rhythm. Six days of work. One day of rest. This rest day is called "Sabbath," which means "to cease." Every six days we are to cease our work and rest. Through this rhythm of six-one, six-one, six-one, we live our lives, do our work, raise our families, gather with our friends, make love to our spouses, eat our food and sleep in our beds. Unfortunately, many of us live in something like a ten-one rhythm—we work ten long, hard days, then try to squeeze in one day off. But we find by that point that we're so tired we can't do anything but collapse. Some of even seek to live in a twelve–one–third rhythm, taking a part of a day—say an afternoon or long morning—off, then re-engaging with the work ahead. But the Sabbath was not created with fractions in mind.

How did we get so terribly lost in a world saturated with striving and grasping, yet somehow bereft of joy and delight?

I suggest that it is this: We have forgotten the Sabbath.[2]

Rhythm Rests on the Hinge of Sabbath

God created the Sabbath, and Sabbath is one of the Ten Commandments. But Sabbath doesn't mean Sunday. Sabbath means to stop what you're doing. When practiced, Sabbath-keeping is an active protest against a culture that is always on, always available and always looking for something else to do. When we practice the ancient rhythm of six days on and one day off, we are saying to the culture around us, "I choose to march to the beat of a different drummer. I am employing the benefit and wonder of a Sabbath rhythm that will restore my life, refuel my soul, and prepare me well for the next week." By practicing Sabbath, we are choosing to be truly countercultural. It is, frankly, an act of resistance.

Does Sabbath-keeping have cultural implications? Absolutely! Sabbath is a way we can redeem both our culture and our time. Rather than closing our garage doors so quickly when we enter our home sanctuaries, Sabbath gives us time to invite a neighbor over for a cup of tea, a time to sit on the patio and linger. Yes, that's it—Sabbath is a time where we can linger, not rush. We hurry and scurry all the other days of the week, but Sabbath lets us eradicate hurry for twenty-four hours of time. Sabbath lets us slow down.

Many of us are tired and worn out, and our churches are led and run by tired and worn-out folks. What if we rested and through our rest became the kind of people that others outside the church wanted to be like? Sabbath could become a subversive tool for church growth. Imagine that!

Living in a Sabbath rhythm helps establish mindfulness instead of mindlessness. We learn to practice the Sabbath, hopefully becoming better and better at knowing what we like to do and what we don't want to do. Sabbath becomes *that* day in the week where we can reflect, ponder and linger with our thoughts. Sabbath holds an inherent promise that we are not machines. We are women and men created in the image of God.

Sabbath has a way of sanctifying time rather than making us feel we have to do more with less. Through a day of Sabbath-keeping, work is put on hold; we engage our hearts and learn to experience a rhythm of anticipated rest.[3]

Natural Time

Our iPhones and Androids wake us up with a vibrating noise that disturbs our sleep. We are "alarmed" to wake up and leave that blissful state of rest. We do that on six days. We have to. For six days we have meetings and obligations. But Sabbath's gift to us is to live by a more natural time than the whip of the clock.

On our working days, there never seems to be enough time. On our days "off" we spiral into doing what we could not accomplish on the other workdays. Sabbath, though, offers us freedom from the yoke that forces us to do more, accomplish more and get "caught up." Sabbath offers us no schedule and no time limits. We linger. We pause. We rise up to gain a different perspective about life and work. There is nothing urgent. There is nothing we have to do. We cease from our list and listmaking. We live and we come alive. This is the gift of Sabbath: we can do what we want when we want to do it. Perhaps you might experiment on Sabbath and not wear a watch. Let your old grandfather clock be "wound up" on Monday. But on Sabbath, let time be more natural. Sleep in. Sip, don't guzzle, your coffee. Find your favorite mug and hold it tight between your hands and breathe. This is how the practice of Sabbath is resistant to time. Sabbath gives us an alternative rhythm by which to live our lives right now and right here.

Here are some benefits of a weekly rhythm of Sabbath keeping:

Our perspective is widened. Through Sabbath keeping we regain a much-needed perspective on life. If we take one day off a week, our view of life softens. We get to come out of the cubicle and the smallness of our lives to say, "Hey, there really is a world outside.

I'm going to enjoy it." Through practicing Sabbath, we have a day where we can hike in the woods, go see a movie, gather with a few life-giving friends, even sleep in late. We begin seeing that there really is more to life than work, more than "another day, another dollar" or whatever mantra you hear and live by. Through ceasing, our view of life grows wide and spacious.

The promise of joy is renewed. God's intent in creating Sabbath was our well-being. The Sabbath was made for us, modeled by God, practiced by Jesus and given to us to enjoy. The Sabbath is God's promise that he cares deeply for us. When we read God's intent for Sabbath in Isaiah, we discover that Sabbath-keeping and joy are directly related.

> If you watch your step on the Sabbath
> and don't use my holy day for personal advantage,
> If you treat the Sabbath as a day of joy,
> God's holy day as a celebration,
> If you honor it by refusing "business as usual,"
> making money, running here and there—
> Then you'll be free to enjoy God! (Isaiah 58:13-14)

In the New International Version that last verse reads, "Then you will find your joy in the Lord."

Joy is fostered in Sabbath rhythm—not in doing as much as we can as fast as we can. With a steady practice of ceasing, we learn that through time and in time we can trickle-charge our hearts. We savor both quality and quantity time with our children and lay down the myth that only quality time matters. We have time, every six days, to engage both emotionally and physically with our children. On Sabbath there is no absentee father or mother because in Sabbath we have time now to engage, to show up and look into the eyes of our children rather than wave goodbye to them as we leave for another day's work. On Sabbath the day's work is not to work, not to use technology, not to be preoccupied with the "what-ifs."

On Sabbath we explore this: What would you like to do *now* that will bring you life? Joy is the soul saying, "I am satisfied. All is well within me. All is well around me. I am experiencing the shalom of God. I am not anxious. I am not worried. I have placed the socks of anxiety and the shoes of worry outside my home for this day. I choose to live in peace. I choose a Sabbath mood to enter my mind, my heart and the space around and within me."

The good news is this: we can experience this shalom—this well-being—every seven days. We anticipate this joy as Sabbath approaches, then we remember this joy as Sabbath is recalled.

Sabbath is God's provision for us to live a resilient life. Sabbath is a provision from God and by God to help us know how to live and how to live well. It's God's idea. It was not developed by corporate America. Actually, quite the opposite is true. Some leading companies such as Chick-Fil-A and Hobby Lobby are standing in the face of culture by closing their business for a twenty-four-hour period of time. The sign on the door of such establishments says, "For the benefit of our employees, we are closed on Sunday." Did you catch that? "For the benefit . . ." Sabbath is a benefit, quite literally "a good thing." However, you don't have to work in a company that promotes Sabbath as a value to practice Sabbath. You can do this in your own work right now.

Sabbath is for our protection. You might be surprised to hear what I am about to tell you, but here it is: There are more verses in the Bible about Sabbath-keeping than about any of the other Ten Commandments. Evidently God knew we would be people who worshiped our work and played at our religion, so to speak. So Sabbath-keeping is a trumpet to sound the alarm, saying, "Are you living and fostering a six-one rhythm? What do you need to cease from this week?"

Ancient Jews put a "Sabbath box" near the table where they would enjoy their weekly Sabbath feast. Into this box they would put objects, symbols of things they wanted to cease from. Some might put in a handful of seeds. Others might put in money. Still others might write down the name of someone they simply wanted and needed to rest from. As the day unfolded, they knew that at the end of Sabbath, the box would be opened and they would take back what they had put in. But the simple aspect of letting go of someone or something was very beneficial.

We have practiced this in our own home. Some Sabbaths I've needed to put my cell phone in the box because I'm so tired of being attached to it. Some Sabbaths I write down a friend's name on a piece of paper and place that paper in the Sabbath box because I need a break from thinking about his or her problem. You may want to place a credit card, car key, house key or other symbol of something you need to rest from. I can assure you that whatever you place in the Sabbath box will be there at the end of the day! Trying this exercise could help protect your mind from being obsessed and consumed so you can be free to rest and find joy.

Sabbath is a wonderful gift to look forward to; it fosters a sense of anticipation. Each Thursday we can know, "Sabbath is coming. I can't wait. I can make it another forty-eight hours." On the other six days we exert, but on Sabbath we receive. We engage for six days, but on the Sabbath we give ourselves permission to disengage. Six-one, six-one, six-one. It is the rhythm we need. And I believe it is the rhythm we all secretly want.

Monthly Rhythm

What could you do each month that would function as an expanded Sabbath? Perhaps you could take two days—a weekend—away. In this expanded time, you could incorporate life-giving activities you enjoy:

- Ride your bike.

- Plant some flowers.

- Write a letter to a relative.

- Invite close friends to enjoy the extended Sabbath.

A monthly rhythm in the workplace could be a day where you allow your team to study, read and explore articles and books that might help the team, the business or simply themselves as individuals. For example, your leadership team could read articles, blogs and books on one of Peter's virtues. Or you could assign monthly topics to explore, such as:

- Is a balanced life possible?

- Are there economic, physical and emotional incentives to experiencing a company- or church-wide Sabbath?

- What would a sabbatical policy look like in our organization?

- What does a healthy workspace actually look like and feel like?

- What are the psychological and spiritual benefits of having time off—time to be "down" and not "up"?

There are many possibilities to explore. Be creative and have fun. Have each person write an executive summary of his or her findings and share it with the others. The executive summary might be this simple: "Here's what I found that was helpful to me," and "Here's what I found that might be helpful for us."

The key here is to think about how one day of caring for your soul could foster more life within you. What can you do this coming month that would bring you life, not drain life from you? Imagine having one day a month dedicated to your own well-being. Imagine having one full day every four weeks intended to let you trickle-charge.

Annual Rhythm

In Jewish culture, eight festivals were to be celebrated every year. These involved good food, dancing and celebration, including worship. In today's rat race, we've removed any notion of an annual anything except maybe a work performance review. But what if this could be rethought?

Sadly, most American workers do not take all of their vacation time. Consider this report from the *Boston Globe*:

> A growing number of North American workers do not take all of their annual allotted days off, companies report. Although some of those days can be rolled over into the next year, workplace analysts estimate that more than half of employees lose at least some vacation every year.
>
> Working nonstop is a "subtle badge of honor" in today's world, said Matt Norquist, general manager at the global workplace consultancy Right Management in New York. Its survey recently found that 70 percent of workers do not use all their vacation time.[4]

This week I'm working with a pastor of a medium-size church in the Midwest. His presenting problem, as he shared on our first day together, was this: "I'm bone-tired. I'm depressed. I have no joy in my life." As we dismantled his "badge of honor" for being such a hard worker, I discovered he had taken only a few days off every year for the past five years. His fatigue had accumulated along with his unused time off. For this pastor, there was no "off." He was only "on."

What about you? How can you take advantage of your time off? How can you plan ahead to use your vacation well? Your vacation is your time to vacate the pressure and demands of work. If you don't take your allotted time off, then you're always "on"—your work never really leaves you, never vacates your subconscious mind. To vacation is to vacate—the schedule, the meetings, the phone calls, the emails—and to be unavailable to anyone.

My wife and I just returned from a vacation on the coast of North Carolina. We stayed on a barrier island, and this island became a metaphor for me as I found myself detaching from work. I noticed a lot of busyness and business on the mainland every time I went across the waterway to the store. As the week unfolded, I didn't venture to the stores. What we had in our cottage became enough. We would do without something if it meant having to go back to the mainland to get it. The island became a much-needed respite—a respite for my soul and for my wife's soul. As we detached from work and the mainland, something deeper happened. We attached to each other. We talked more. We often sat wordless, staring at the sunset. We connected as we disconnected. And this connection was restorative and redemptive.

Sabbatical Rhythm

A sabbatical is an extended Sabbath, a time of replenishment before the next stretch of one's career. While sabbaticals are well-known in educational circles, they are not familiar in corporate and especially ministry circles. A sabbatical is a three- to twelve-month window of time where you can rest, disengage, do something totally different and embark on courses or retreats that will equip and enable you to go the long haul.

In agriculture, no farmer in his right mind would plant and reap every single year without a break. No, the wise farmer allows the land to rest—to replenish itself by lying fallow, receiving rich nutrients into the soil so that after the sabbatical of rest, the land is ready to produce again.

One of the main reasons churches and companies do not employ the sabbatical rhythm is that we hold to the lie that people are indispensible and we simply cannot do without that person or position. But by engaging a sabbatical rhythm in our work culture, we acknowledge that no one is indispensible: "Go! Have your time. You'll be better for it and, when you come back, we will be better for it."

A sabbatical has its own rhythm. Part of a sabbatical should be for rest. In the initial phase you prioritize rest. You sleep well, eat well and laugh well. Part of a sabbatical should be for renewal. In the renewing phase of your sabbatical, plan on participating in a spiritual retreat, a course on some topic of interest, or a seminar where you can experience something new, something that helps you grow and learn. A final phase of a healthy sabbatical is to retool ourselves in some way. As lifelong learners, we need to participate in our own reeducation and development. As I prepare for my own sabbatical next year, I want to take a course from a nearby community college where I can learn about real estate. I've always been interested in buying and selling homes, so I figure why not learn more? Why not retool myself in an area of keen interest?

As you consider a daily, weekly, monthly and annual rhythm, you will discover that no one is going to hijack your life but yourself. You really do have the power and the choice to care for yourself and for those you love by living in rhythm—a rhythm that will give you the greatest gift you can give yourself—the ability to live your life in a sustainable and resilient way. Rhythm is the way to live the life that is good and the life that is desirable!

8

THE LEADER'S LIMITS

Saying No in Order to Live Yes

◆ ◆ ◆

Let me say it as plainly as I can. It is a myth to believe that:

- People can be whoever they want to be.
- People can do whatever they want to do.
- People can reach for the stars and grab them.
- People can achieve whatever they set their mind to achieve.

And then there is this myth:

- You need to give 110 percent all the time!

I know, I know. I stand in the face of positive thinking, the American dream, and that whole realm of possibilities to say such a thing. But it's true. To hold to such myths is to hold to a lie. I've been able to travel to many different countries and see many different people groups all trying to make a living and eke out a wage and eat their daily bread. I've found that it's really only Americans who hold to such notions of wishful thinking. In my work with leaders, this wishful thinking is often the topic of our private conversations when their dreams die or they hit the walls that prevent them from living, or being, or doing whatever they wanted.

Simply put, you and I are not God. Only God is boundless in his ability to be and do. God is unlimited in terms of space, time, availability, energy and passion. Since we are not God, then learning to live within our limits is key to living a good life. To embrace lies and myths that overpromise and underdeliver sets us up for failure and months, years—even a lifetime—of disappointment.

In our dreams and in the pages of fiction, we read about a life without limits: having all the sex we want; having more money than we can dream of; skiing in the Winter Olympics; and finding, having and holding what no person has discovered yet. But men and women are limited in their time—we have only so many hours we can give and work. We are limited in terms of availability—we need margin, boundaries and space. We are limited in having healthy relationships—social scientists say twelve close relationships are possible while we can maintain about a hundred at a distance. We are limited in our energy—we are not always boundless and able to do anything at any time. Our passion also hits limits in terms of the effects of aging and wear and tear on our bodies.

Facing Our Limits

Did you ever want to play football in the NFL or have your son play? Do you know the likelihood of that happening? Here's what the website for the NFL says about that very scenario. Read closely:

> While many young people every year set their goals on becoming NFL players, it is extremely difficult to reach that level. Statistically of the 100,000 high school seniors who play football every year, only 215 will ever make an NFL roster. That is 0.2%! Even of the 9,000 players that make it to the college level only 310 are invited to the NFL scouting combine,

the pool from which teams make their draft picks. As you can see, most people who want to become NFL players will not. Therefore it is very important to come up with alternative plans for the future.[1]

Sobering. I find it intriguing that the website for the NFL Players Association states these stats and encourages young people to come up with alternative plans for the future. I suppose it's their way of saying that every aspiring football player needs to truly embrace limitations.

Before you think, "Hey, this author is being cruel. Where's the love?" let me say that by embracing your own limitations, you will be free to live in the real world with expectations and desires anchored in reality. Such freedom fosters a life that is not only worth living but that has the inner marks of satisfaction, happiness and fulfillment. Let me explain how this happens.

The Truth Sets You Free

I love the words of Jesus when he tells his followers, "The truth will set you free" (John 8:32 NIV). Freedom comes by embracing the truth, not by holding onto lies, illusions and myths.

It's interesting to note that the apostle Paul wrote two different books to the same group of followers of Jesus in a city named Corinth in the Greek Isles. In the second book, we see an older, more mature Paul talk about living within limits. In 2 Corinthians 10:13, Paul explains his understanding of living within the limits God has set for us. He writes about not overextending ourselves: "We, however, will not boast beyond proper limits, but will confine our boasting to the sphere of service God himself has assigned to us, a sphere that also includes you" (NIV). *The Message* puts it this way: "We aren't making outrageous claims here. We're sticking to the limits of what God has set for us."

A limit requires a basic understanding of where you should invest yourself and where you should refrain. A limit is understanding what writer Wendell Berry calls your "carrying capacity." How much should you work? Not how long *can* you work, but how long *should* you work? And it's not just about work. Limits are important in most aspects of our lives. How much should we exercise, eat, sleep, play and use technology? How much can we carry before something gets dropped?

What's true is this: A person cannot give 110 percent all the time. It's just not possible. As the Bible says, "Even youths grow tired and weary" (Isaiah 40:30 NIV). Even young men and women need to learn the limitations of their physical strength. Tim's spouse told me, "All I get from Tim when he gets home are the leftovers." It's a message my wife, Gwen, tried to tell me when my own career was blossoming and I was at the zenith of my vocational ladder. Now, years later, I lament to Gwen and often share in my talks, "I gave the best years of my life to my work and the leftovers to my family." Sure, I tried to be present, to go to my son's basketball games and soccer matches. I tried to understand the concept of "quality time." But now I can say that while I was physically present, I was far, far away in some distant land in my mind. I was emotionally absent. I was checked out, preoccupied with planning meetings, building reports and strategies for growth—in other words, my own kingdom.

I regret not really showing up for much of my life. I showed up in work but not in other ways, and I paid the price. Please hear me—so will you. No one escapes the boomerang of ignoring your limits. I have spent much time seeking to regain the "years the locusts have eaten" (Joel 2:25)[2] with my family ties and especially with my most sacred of all relationships—my wife. Learning to live within my limits was an "aha" moment for me. When the lights came on, my life began to change—and so will yours, all for the better.

Exceeding Output

Overextending yourself is stretching your physical, emotional, financial, vocational and relational boundaries to the point of depletion. Have you ever heard the expression someone says when the money is running tight? It goes like this: "There's too much month left at the end of the money." Translated this means, "I've run out of money to pay all my bills and it's only the middle of the month." That's what happens when we overextend ourselves; there's more asked of us than we can give.

This overextending causes stress to accumulate: the stress at home, in the workplace, during travel—it all piles up like a huge stack of dirty laundry. Stress, as we all know, is deadly to our health. Every doctor and therapist will tell you that unresolved stress will "do you in." Stress works itself out through our blood pressure and attacks our vital organs. Stress releases a toxin that when built up leaves its marks inside of us. We live with a tyranny of the urgent that drives us, manipulates us and sucks passion right out of our marrow and veins. Everything must be done now. Everything has to be quick.

Professions that call for a high emotional investment in people, otherwise known as "helping professions," need to take note. Examples include ministers, counselors, social workers, nurses, doctors and teachers. The principle that anyone involved in a helping profession needs to uphold is this: Those who care must be cared for. No one is the exception to this, not even you! An important step in learning to live your life within limits is to confess, "There are no exceptions to this principle. Not even me!"

In the military, men and women who have repeated deployments where they live in harm's way for extended periods apart from loved ones experience signs and symptoms of the burnout and depletion I am describing. I have three sons who serve as officers in the US Army. When they are deployed, I see firsthand the stress on their wives and children and in their own souls. I also sense my own stress rising when they are deployed. Sometimes I can't sleep if I know they are truly in harm's way.

I've worked with numerous people who work in disaster relief and crisis situations for large organizations. After flying overseas or traveling to a site where a hurricane, earthquake or human plight has developed, they go into fierce action mode, doing everything possible to save lives and alleviate suffering. It always takes a toll. One relief worker who is employed by a United Nations relief agency came to our retreat and introduced himself with these words: "I'm DOA—dead on arrival. I'm spent and have no idea where I left my heart along the way."

Preventive Care

Most people in the developed world know to wash their hands before eating. By washing your hands, you are preventing the spread of germs that can make you sick. In developing countries, many crosscultural workers will teach people about drinking water that is safe. They say, "Urinate over there and keep this area clean and pure so nothing bad will go into the water." It's a simple truth that helps keep people healthy. Learning to live within your limits is a simple preventive principle that will help you stay healthy. All aspects of caring for yourself are really preventive work. Preventive care is an important part of the work within the work. It's never a selfish act to care for yourself. Never! In the bigger picture of life and health it is stewardship.

To explore your own limits, consider these strategies that will help you as you begin setting realistic limits for yourself.

First, consider how you can conserve your energy. Learn some conservation skills. You simply cannot give all your energy all the time. No one ever told me this. I was taught to give my all and that my all was needed, if not demanded. I was also taught via sermons,

books and stories that even God expected my all. Now I know this
is simply not true. Even Jesus did not even begin his thirty-six-
month mission on earth until he was thirty years old. With the kind
of thinking ingrained in me, I found myself wondering why: "Jesus
wasted a lot of time. What if he had begun earlier in life—hung up
his tool belt by age eighteen and started out then? Look at how
much more he could have done!"

Winston Churchill, one of the most undeniably significant
leaders of the free world, has much to teach emerging leaders about
the "know before you go" principle. In Paul Johnson's biography of
this legendary British hero, we read these words:

> In 1946, I had the good fortune to ask him a question:
> "Mr. Churchill, sir, to what do you attribute your success
> in life?"
> Without pause or hesitation, he replied:
> "Conservation of energy. Never stand up when you can sit
> down, and never sit down when you can lie down."[3]

Johnson goes on to explain the idea of conserving energy on an
everyday basis:

> Churchill was capable of tremendous physical and intellectual
> efforts, of high intensity over long periods, often with little
> sleep. But he had corresponding powers of relaxation, filled
> with a variety of pleasurable occupations, and he also had the
> gift of taking short naps when time permitted. Again, when
> possible, he spent his mornings in bed, telephoning, dictating,
> and receiving visitors.[4]

Second, embrace the idea of living life in rhythm, not in balance.
As we have already seen, the idea of balance is a lie. It simply cannot
be maintained. Despite all the seminars, books and TED Talks,
balance is bunk. Rhythm is doable and allows you to develop an

understanding of living life within limits. I have a friend who is a registered nurse in a cancer ward at a leading hospital. She works three days on, four days off. Her three days on are twelve-hour shifts that sometimes extend to thirteen hours—even fourteen when much documentation is necessarily. Her first day off is useless to her. She is so tired, so exhausted, so spent that she told me, "On my first day off I'm no good to anyone. I just sleep, 'veg' and eat. By the second day off, I'm sensing who I am again and go out for lunch or dinner with a good friend." It's a necessary rhythm that she has come to understand about her own life and need for recovery.

Third, steward your output by mentally and emotionally disengaging after you work. I coach leaders to leave their work at work and not to do work at home if at all possible. If you work at home, define a definite workspace. (Hint—this should not be your bedroom.) In defining a distinct work area, you create mental and emotional space.

My wife and I do not chat about people we work with, discuss issues relating to work or even mention the names of our teammates on our days off or in our home after work hours. We've set high boundaries here and we limit our conversations to issues pertaining to us; our kids, grandkids and close friends; and vacation plans. We try to set our minds to ease by saying, "This is not a Sabbath conversation. Let's talk about this tomorrow."

After every great output of energy, plan and schedule a time for input. Give yourself what brings you life. Give yourself permission to live and not just work. After you spend enormous time and energy on a project or travel obligation, know that you need recovery time. You cannot simply give and give and give. This is a deadly mistake that will lead to burnout and depression. You have to replenish.

I travel internationally and after doing this for several years, I've learned that these trips—the changing of time zones, the stress of waiting and delays and security issues—require that I set aside calendar time to recoup. Last year I traveled to India. I flew all night and half of the next day to get there. I arrived and was whisked away in a taxi to give a talk. It was one of the biggest mistakes of my life. I was completely zoned out. Now I know better. I "know before I go" and build in a day or two to get adjusted, to rest and to have time to collect my thoughts.

After a time of intense work, how about taking a couple of days for yourself—to go see a sight or to have some life-giving experience? Could your spouse join you for an extended time off knowing that you've been "on" so much lately? By thinking like this, you will insulate yourself from the crisis of cramming too much in and doing too much. Build in your time off before you go. Work this out with your boss and team and call it "compensatory time" or something that will give you permission to take good care of yourself. This is vital to learning to live within your limits.

Fourth, face the truth that you cannot do everything and do everything well. We cannot burn the candle at both ends. Jesus asked three penetrating questions of his followers—not people who were considering following him, but those who had already signed up. His questions were:

- Are you tired?

- Are you worn out?

- Are you burned out on religion? (See Matthew 11:28)

These three questions give us permission to know our limits, to grow in our awareness of how we are really doing and to care for our souls. Many people are living in one of these three unhealthy spheres that Jesus describes: physical exhaustion, mental anguish involving guilt and shame for not doing more, and the big one: being burned out—that state where we live like we're fried without the hope of recovery.

Burnout

Burnout is a state of mental or physical exhaustion caused by excessive and prolonged stress. The key word here is stress. There are several identifiable stages of burnout.[5] (See if you have at least two of the symptoms from any of the following lists.)

Stage one: stress arousal

- Persistent irritability
- Persistent anxiety
- Periods of high blood pressure
- Insomnia
- Forgetfulness
- Heart palpitations
- Inability to concentrate
- Frequent headaches

Stage two: energy conservation

- Lateness for work
- Procrastination
- Needed three day weekends
- Decreased sexual desire
- Persistent tiredness in the mornings
- Social withdrawing from family and friends
- Cynical attitudes
- Apathy
- Change in eating and drinking habits

Stage three: exhaustion

- Chronic sadness or depression

- Chronic stomach/bowel issues
- Chronic physical fatigue
- The desire to drop out of work and society
- The desire to move away from friends and family
- Suicidal thoughts

The answer to burnout is not simply rest. We must look more deeply at issues that are causing the stress that leads to a constant state of fatigue. Often these are embedded in our stories. We find that when we are close to burnout, a weekend away seems like more work and effort, so we'd just rather not go. The truth is there are issues in our past—patterns, modeling and beliefs—that must be unpacked and examined to understand why we are living in such a way. Why is it so hard to simply be kind to ourselves? It's wise for us to examine our drive to perform as well as our need to be significant and successful. As we do we note patterns and seasons where issues tend to rise and surface and then wane. It is especially wise to track sadness and grief. Another very real component of burnout is its physical toll on our bodies. The prolonged wear and tear on our bodies must be addressed with a physician, athletic trainer, life coach or spiritual director.

Burnout does not happen in twenty-four hours. Perhaps not even in one long, hard, demanding week. It happens little by little over time. It is the steady slow leak in the tire that finally goes flat—incapable of going around one more time, no matter how slowly you move. You just have to stop.

The Remedy for Burnout

What many people don't realize is that when someone experiences burnout, it takes a long, long time for them to come back to life. A day off, a weekend away or a short vacation will not attend to the soul of the one who is truly spent, gone, flat and burned out to the core of his or her being. There is no remedy for coming back to life other than time, love and (I believe) beauty. It simply takes lots of time for a person to come back from the brink. It may require many conversations, much-needed time in solitude and quiet, and more. As busy people, we make the mistake of trying to hurry up our burnout recovery. By slowing down and embracing what can happen only in time and through time, we accept a God-given reality that we cannot microwave. Time heals and that is simply the fact of the matter.

Love is crucial because burned-out people need a place where they are accepted, not expected to say anything or pray any scripted prayers. To love someone who has hit a wall or is dealing with burnout is to accept them just as they are. It is to avoid stating what *you* think is needed and how long *you* think the recovery should take. There is no cookie-cutter way to program someone's personal resurrection. While Jesus' own resurrection took three days to happen, yours and mine is probably going to take longer.

Beauty has a way of reviving the soul and inspiring the heart. But the corporate world and the modern church have lost the power of beauty in our work and worship. We sit in cubicles and we worship by the light of technology. We no longer need candles—they seem such a waste. Our modern church buildings are constructed to keep the natural light out so that we can see projections on screens. Office buildings are designed to be functional—which is necessary, but at what expense? Common places bring workers together to have conversation, to share ideas, to connect and be human in their work. What if we thought more about how to bring beauty to common areas through art, design, color and texture?

The ancients believed that nature was the "second book of God"—the Bible being the first. Nature revives us when we walk the trails, sit in the parks, watch the flowers and birds, and breathe. Simone

Weil was a French young woman who lived in the terrible era of World War II in her home country. She knew of the power of beauty to resurrect the heart. She lamented that "there are only two things that pierce the human soul. One is affliction. The other is beauty."[6]

Most of you will be able to quickly recall a hike you took on some mountain trail, a walk you took on some desolate beach, an excursion you had in a garden. You know intuitively what I am telling you here: beauty helps. It helps more than we know. Leonardo da Vinci, the great Italian artist and genius said, "The ministers to the soul are the five senses." Where all five senses are not engaged, we simply have no ministry to our souls.

Perhaps you could take a moment now to envision a more beautiful workspace—realizing how important it is and how much time you spend in that space. Pull your team or group of friends together to have this conversation: "What place does beauty have in the space that we work in each day?" That question alone will get a deeper conversation started, I can assure you.

One of the reasons I trust and respect the Bible so much is that it never attempts to hide the mistakes of the leaders we read about and the lessons they had to learn. It's remarkable to see how many biblical personalities experienced symptoms of burnout: Abraham, David, Elijah and Paul, to name a few. Paul confesses the dark night of his own soul in 2 Corinthians, where he despaired of life and felt "the sentence of death" (2 Corinthians 1:9 NIV). In his work Paul was passionate about starting churches and evangelizing those who were truly lost in life. But after so much work, so much stress and so much giving, he tells us, he hit a wall: "We had no rest, but we were harassed at every turn—conflicts on the outside, fears within" (2 Corinthians 7:5 NIV). What helped Paul is what might help us. He needed time with his friend Titus. Time with his dear friend would prove to be life-giving, not life-draining. Paul needed "Titus time." Who is the person you can be with, talk to and receive encouragement from? Who fills you and does not drain you? Do you have a regular time set up to simply be with this life-giving friend?

As I've said, I like the apostle Paul more as an older man than I like him as a young man. In his youth he was a zealot. He lived hard. He believed hard and some of his actions before his conversion to following the ways of Jesus were horrendous.[7]

But in 2 Corinthians 2 we read Paul's account of realizing that God had opened a door for Paul, presenting a new opportunity. He was free to walk through this open door of possibility and take his work to a new level. But we read this:

> Now when I went to Troas to preach the gospel of Christ and found that the Lord had opened a door for me, I still had no peace of mind, because I did not find my brother Titus there. So I said goodbye to them and went on to Macedonia. (2 Corinthians 2:12-13 NIV)

Paul realized his limits. He needed to be with Titus—his longtime and trusted friend. The journey had been hard, demanding and relentless. There were challenges everywhere. Paul puts it this way:

> For when we came into Macedonia, we had no rest, but we were harassed at every turn—conflicts on the outside, fears within. But God, who comforts the downcast, comforted us by the coming of Titus, and not only by his coming but also by the comfort you had given him. He told us about your longing for me, your deep sorrow, your ardent concern for me, so that my joy was greater than ever. (2 Corinthians 7:5-7 NIV)

Paul stopped. Instead of doing more work he deliberately chose to do less work, and that fostered his own resilience. Titus gave him what few others could. He provided the safety of a trusted friend who could ask good questions and listen well.

As you explore your own limits, remember you are doing the

Inside Job. Connect the dots of your past with your present. In exploring your limits and capacity and then setting your limits, you are ensuring yourself much-needed space and grace not only to be good to yourself but to be good to those around you. But it starts with you. Give yourself permission to live a life of limits. You can't do it all. You were never meant to. But you can do what matters.

Doing your own Inside Job means looking at your rhythm as well as facing and knowing your limits. As you grow in the apostle Peter's virtue of "knowledge" in each one of these vital areas, you will be able to catch yourself in the act when you feel breathless, sense the stress within that you can't get it all done and more. As you learn to catch yourself in the act, you live more sanely and live with your own well-being in mind.

9

THE LEADER'S TRANSITIONS

Understanding Change

◆◆◆

It's been said that the only constant in life is change. While that's pithy and true, it's not always reassuring. Change, as William Bridges explains it, is "situational: the move to a new site, the retirement of the founder, the reorganization of the roles on a team."[1] Change is the ending of a relationship, the death of a parent, the move of your best friend. Any change brings with it a gap, something called a transition. These in-between times are hard, even in the best of circumstances, because they represent moving from one phase of life to another. Think about moving into a new house—even if you're thrilled at the prospect of a new place to live, there's still a lot of work to be done between the old home and your new digs.

Transitions are a new normal in today's quick-changing world. And transitions are different from change. Change is situational and external, while a transition is the process of internal adjustment to that change.[2] Transition is the inside stuff—the inside work, the Inside Job we need to attend to in order to leave clean and begin well in the next season.

For example, an in-between time is when you sense you're ready to leave one job and start the search to find the next. In this new space, you sense, intuit or awaken to the realization that something is going to change. You may not know the specifics, but you know some kind of alteration to life is in the air. Of course, at other times we do know the details: we're diagnosed with a life-threatening illness, a relationship hits a dead end or upper management announces an organizational change that leaves us updating our résumé.

There are many different kinds of transitions: the time between graduating from college and beginning your first real job, the season between being single and being married, the anxiety in transitioning from the second child to the third—something most parents agree they're never fully prepared for (when we had our third son, we realized we had to switch from man-to-man to a zone style of parenting). There is the mental process of transitioning to a new job with greater responsibilities while missing your previous team where trust had been established and everyone knew what to do and what was expected.

Missionaries, expatriates and crosscultural workers transition when they leave one country to live in another. There's a new language, a new city to get used to, new customs and new food. There is also missing the culture you just left and the people you loved there. Then there's the new house, new church, new neighborhood and new school for your children. All of these external changes stir up our insides. Our bodies are affected. Our sleep becomes interrupted. Our fuse gets short and, if we're not careful, we can explode, causing a mess that's sometimes difficult to clean up. Every move, every new position, every new office setting, every new relationship or end of a long, established one brings with it this time of transition.

I remember a pivotal moment of transition when I took my firstborn son to college. I dreaded that moment. He wanted to go far away from home while we wanted him to choose a school closer to us in Colorado. When the day arrived for him to move into his room, we hauled in boxes and with each box lifted from my car trunk, my heart sank lower. I was anticipating our final goodbye, and I feared it. Would I lose it in the hallway and sob like a baby? Would he lose it? As the moment drew near, I planned a quick escape. I said, "Blake, this is the moment. I need to get out of here or I might break down." I was halfway joking about it but my son knew this outburst of emotion on my end was a distinct possibility.

Anxious for me *not* to break down, he said, "Let's walk to the car." We did. We embraced. I was okay—happy and sad and full of hope and anxiety, missing him already but glad he would have the opportunity for so many new experiences. Blake walked off and I got into the car and shut the door. Then I lost it. That moment is etched in me clearly as a passage into Blake's manhood and a passage in my life as a parent learning to let go. It was definitely a moment of paradox.

The Place of Paradox

Paradox is a great word for describing a time of transition. All of a sudden your soul has to host mixed feelings and emotions, and not just one at a time but in a flood of opposition. They often topple you over. I am reminded of Charles Dickens's *A Tale of Two Cities*. He opens the novel this way:

> It was the best of times, it was the worst of times, it was the age of wisdom, it was the age of foolishness, it was the epoch of belief, it was the epoch of incredulity, it was the season of Light, it was the season of Darkness, it was the spring of hope, it was the winter of despair, we had everything before us, we had nothing before us, we were all going direct to Heaven, we were all going direct the other way.[3]

Dickens describes well the paradox of transition, of being in between two realities. This in-between is another place for the Inside Job, for the work within the work.

Brett and Nan had moved several times internationally. Each time their company said, "Move," they moved. After the fifth time, Brett and Nan considered themselves experts in transitions. Nan shared a story with me from when they moved to Thailand. This move required a new house, a new school, new friends, a new workspace for Brett and a whole new team that he did not know. Upon settling in, Nan went to the market to purchase some things for their new home. While there she found another expat woman learning against a wall in the back of the store. The woman looked like she was in a daze and perhaps needed assistance. Nan asked if she was okay and the woman said, "I'm so overwhelmed. I don't know what end is up. I don't speak the language. I hate the smells here and I just want to go home. I feel as if I have just been cut adrift and I'm about to hit a big sandbar."

Nan recognized the state this woman was in at that particular moment. She knew that daze well. She invited the woman to tea and as they sat down the woman began to pour her heart out to Nan. As the tears flowed, Nan simply listened and gave the woman space and time to get it out—the messiness of transition, the collision of the inner world with the external world.

Soldiers, aviators and sailors all face massive transition issues when they are deployed, fight in a war or skirmish and then transition back home. The solider has been in harm's way. The adrenalin has been high, the pressure enormous. Perhaps he or she has witnessed terrible scenes creating horrifying memories. Where does that stress go? How does a person process what is tearing them up on the inside?

As recently as World War II, soldiers were shipped home literally on a ship. The trip across the oceans would last weeks. In those weeks of crossing the ocean, the soldiers could tell their stories, sharing their nightmares and close calls in the battle. They slept, ate and talked. They had their comrades to listen to them. They cried. They talked. They were able to debrief in storytelling. It was a forced time of transition that benefitted those soldiers who were open to it.

But consider how it is these days. In a matter of hours a soldier who has been in a hot zone can find himself or herself in a commercial airport waiting to fly across several time zones and a dozen countries. There is no time to decompress, no time to adjust, no time to get grounded in the new realities. The in-between time is hours, not weeks—and certainly not months.

As I write this, one of my sons is deployed with his special forces unit overseas. He has been overseas for four months. He not only left us, his parents (can you tell I love my kids?), but his beautiful wife, Sara, and their newborn daughter, Caroline. It's been a long season for Sara to be alone, parent alone and go through a harsh Colorado winter alone. And then there is all that Jordan is missing in Caroline's life: her first smile, her first time sitting up, her first time to eat with a spoon and a whole lot more first times. Jordan will return in two weeks. Another transition will begin. Jordan and Sara will together be in a time of transition when Jordan holds his daughter for the first time in months. Will Caroline have a meltdown in the airport—not from the joy of seeing her daddy but from not knowing who the big strong man is who's kissing, squeezing and hugging her too much?

Rare is the church or sending organization that helps a missionary family in transition. Expectations are established that the work is what counts. This has led to devastating statistics in mission organizations forced to look at their retention rates for missionaries who simply are not prepared for the long, hard and challenging transition to life in a new culture, or the transition that takes place when the missionary comes back home. Few missionaries are allowed to process what happened inside them as they did their outside work. Churches and agencies are eager to hear reports of growth, but what about the internal chaos happening in the life of the one who was sent?

In the book *Stuck*, author Terry Walling writes, "Transitions serve to bring about needed change, provide clarity in life direction, consolidate learning, deepen values, shift the paradigm and advance one's influence and/or ministry."[4] The feeling of being "stuck" is what we want to avoid. A transition season offers lessons we can learn that can transform us, help us and help the people we love who are living life without us.

Discharging the Loyal Soldier

Richard Rohr, a popular author and Franciscan priest, writes of our need to help explore creative transitions this way:

> At the end of [World War II], some Japanese communities had the wisdom to understand that many of their returning soldiers were not fit or prepared to reenter civil, peaceful society. The veterans' only identity for their formative years had been as a "loyal soldier" to their country. They needed a broader identity to rejoin their communities and families. You do not know how to be a father/mother or a brother/ sister or a husband/wife with a soldier persona. They are completely different identities.
>
> So the Japanese created a ceremony whereby a soldier was publicly thanked and praised for his service to the people. After the soldier had been profusely honored, an elder would stand and announce with authority: "The war is now over! The community needs you to let go of what has well served you and us up to now. But we now need you to return as a man, a father, a husband, and something beyond a soldier."
>
> We have no such rites of passage in our ritual-starved

culture, and they are deeply needed to let go of a past marriage, a past identity, or a past failure. Otherwise, we just keep living, regretting, or trying to redo our past over and over again.[5]

When one of our sons was honorably discharged from active-duty service in the US Army, Gwen and I felt the need to help him transition. We asked his friends and family to write letters of appreciation—notes of welcoming him back into life as a civilian. We gathered together and honored our son with a wooden box holding all the letters written for him to read, savor and think though in his transition time. It was simple, yet it was a profound way to help our son transition well.

Companies and churches would do well to honor the loyal worker who has served hard and long. In blessing someone for his or her faithful service and releasing that person to the next step on the journey is to help a goodbye become more than a hug or handshake and a walk to the door. To honor someone is to truly love them. To thank workers for their service is to give dignity to the work and to the giving of so much of themselves through the work.

The Sacred Space of In-Between

"So much of this life is lived in between, between the now and the not yet, between arriving and departing, between growing up and growing old, between questions and answers. Lord, help us not to live for the distant day when the in-between will be no more, but help us to have the courage to step into that sacred space of the in-between—knowing that this is a place where life is transformed."[6]

These are the words of Jim Branch, a former leader with Young Life, a Christian organization that works with high school students. Branch became a student of the transition process himself when one job ended and a new phase of life began. These words were not easy to write but he did earn them honestly, by learning the experience of transitions.

Let me state again the definition of transition. A transition is the process of internal adjustments to external changes.[7] Did you catch that? A transition is a *process*—it's not a one-time thing. Learning about transitions and managing your own transitions is your Inside Job. To know about the in-between times is to empower yourself so there are no surprises. You learn to be extremely good to yourself in times of upheaval. You take the extra time necessary because you have realized you are not in a race. This is a journey you are on—a marathon with many unexpected turns and twists in the path ahead. You give up the myth that you can manage this upcoming change once and for all. No, we're all different. Everyone will process the transition in a different way and at a different speed. The key is to know this—and to extend grace to yourself and everyone who is transitioning with you. Let me ask you a question: What would it look like for you to be excessively gentle with yourself if you find yourself in a time of transition right now? If you read on to the next paragraph, you're busted! See, we do everything fast—even our reading. Stop. Pause. Reflect and pray.

The process involves time, adjustment, recalculation and perhaps even a turn in a different direction. It's not instant. It doesn't happen just because you showed up somewhere new. Some transitions may be easier to navigate—for example, many companies that ask people to move help their workers relocate. But I'm not aware of many that help you navigate all of the change that is happening inside of you—and that will continue to surface for a long time.

Tom and Mary live all their married life overseas. The built a house overseas, had three children overseas and worked in Europe for eighteen years. They were returning to the United States (transition number one) because Tom's parents were aging (transition number two) and their children were all in new seasons of schooling (transition number three). Tom and Mary came to us for five days of inside work, what we call a "soul care intensive." It was five days of taking, sharing, digging into their hearts and helping them wake up to what was about to happen to them and in them as they move "home" (transition number four). As we explored their transitions in the above categories, Tom's eyes got bigger and bigger. He was sobered. He had never thought of coming home as being such a big deal. They were fluent in Romanian and would now only use English (transition number five). They had rarely seen or used a debit card and were unaccustomed to large supermarkets and multiplex theaters (transition number six). I gave Tom more sobering news when I said, "Tom, it's likely going to take you four to five years before you feel like home is really home."

Tom didn't like this news. After all, he was an American wanting a quick fix. I've followed Tom and Mary's story for seven years now. I see them every year and we joke about that conversation because Tom now knows I was right. The longer you live and work in one place, the longer it will take to feel like you're home when you switch to a new place.

In working in depth with so many marketplace leaders as well as leaders involved in ministry, I generally tell people: for every year you've spent in one place doing one thing and living in one house, expect one month of transition time to help you adjust mentally, emotionally, physically and relationally (and remember, all these categories are spiritual). If you work in one job for twelve years, it will take you around twelve months to feel stable and have a sense of belonging.

I'm writing this in a little cottage on a beach on the coast of North Carolina. Friends stopped by the other day and gave us a framed picture as a gift. They knew we were here for me to have dedicated space to write this book. They also knew the beach was important to us. Gwen and I dated at this beach. We had our second son while vacationing at this beach (Gwen went into labor early). We vacationed here for years and this is the place our children know and love. The framed quote is this: "You can shake the sand from your shoes but it never leaves your soul!"

That quote is perhaps the best way for me to explain how important it is to navigate transitions. Tom and Mary's feet had the dust of Romania on them. Ours have the sand of the beach. Yours may have the scree of the mountains. This truth needs to be honored and not denied. We must honor where we've been in order to wholeheartedly begin the next phase of our journey. This requires time, adjustment and getting used to a new way of doing life. This is what happens in the sacred space of in-between. When these deep influences from our story are not honored, our souls will experience violence in transition. When we move too fast and think we can just show up in our new place and start right away, we are violating the sacred space of the in-between time. We're not gaining the wisdom and insight we can learn from what just happened. We're counting coup and getting on with it.

Your Baggage Is Waiting

They call it "baggage"—all the stuff we take with us when we move from one place to another. This is obviously literal, but it's also figurative. Our baggage during a transition can spill out of our boxes and trip up our lives at the oddest times—often when we least expect it. Feelings, grief, depression mingled with excitement combined with joy, and the anticipation of a new beginning can all collide.

You've left a place that was important, whether you liked it or not. The people living there and the work you did influenced you. You experienced the good, the bad and the ugly of it all. It can make you cry and it can make you laugh. But here's the thing—your baggage is always there and it usually doesn't wait until you have time to deal with it. Transitions don't work that way. Life doesn't work that way.

William Bridges has given us a wonderful tool to help us understand the inner work that is needed when we go through a transition time.[8] Bridges describes this in three phases:

- *Letting go.* This is the place where we deal with the losses of our lives, work, family, relationships, church and more.

- *The neutral zone.* This is the place of chaos. The place of crisis. Crisis means a "dangerous opportunity."

- *The new beginning.* New place. New relationship. New opportunity. New identity.

The illustration of a bridge is helpful to envision this important insight.

When you walk across the bridge of a transition, you first leave the shore. You leave the place where you've been and you see the other side—but you're not on the other side yet. You're on a bridge. You've just started to move across. This is the "letting go"—this is the beginning of a transition. As you keep moving forward, you reach the middle of the bridge. You've made progress. You can see what you've left but you're also aware that you still haven't arrived.

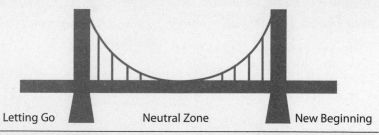

Letting Go   Neutral Zone   New Beginning

Figure 2. Phases of transition

It's going to take more time. This is the "neutral zone"—a kind of no-man's land. Finally you reach the other side, the "new beginning." You find yourself missing some of the past—maybe the food, the people, the culture—but you're ready to explore the new adventure. It's time to begin again.

The bridge spans two different realities in your life—two different worlds sometimes. And all the space in the middle is chaos. Chaos can be frightening, debilitating, paralyzing, threatening. It can also be the stirrings of a brave new adventure. Chaos has within it all the dangerous possibilities that cause us both to fear the unknown and also to find the courage to forge a way through it. We can walk forward in an attitude of blessing and expectation or we can walk in an attitude of feeling cursed and see ourselves as victims of what happened "over there." Doing the work within the work will help you be aware of what's happening inside you as you prepare for the phase of the journey.

We might think with our modern mindset that we are the only victims of change. Perhaps this is simply a new phenomenon of living in a fast-paced world. Wrong! The Bible records the spiritual journeys of many men and women who experienced significant transition. William Bridges's book was not yet out when Moses left the court of Pharaoh, where he was a privileged and highly regarded leader. Moses might have benefited from Bridges's chart of the stages of transition. But what Moses called it was entirely different: he experienced a wilderness. As we read the Bible through the lens of transition, we find many examples of men and women navigating transition times.

- Moses: Forty years in the wilderness.

- Joseph: Betrayed by his brothers and also by Pharaoh, then imprisoned.

- Ruth and Naomi: Their world changed in the death of their husbands.

- David: Vocational shift from shepherd to warrior to king.

- Paul: After his conversion spent three years in the desert of Arabia.

- Jesus: Forty days in the wilderness after beginning his public ministry.

- Peter: Vocational transition from fishing for fish to fishing for people.

Simply imagine the transition these biblical personalities went through.

In conclusion, here are ten guidelines to remember when you are in a transition season of life.

1. Use the bridge analogy. Point out on the bridge where you've been and where you are headed. The middle section of the bridge is your time of chaos—it's helpful to call it what it is. "Chaos" is a good word that helps reduce the illusion that you're across the bridge when you're not. Call it "chaos" and let all the feelings of chaos come to the surface. (The workbook has ideas here to help you envision what this might look like in your life or the life of your company.)

2. Be intentional in the chaos season by using the language with your spouse, team, children and friends. When someone asks you, "How are you doing?" describe the bridge. Tell them you are not fully across yet and you sense it's going to take longer— perhaps a lot longer than you expected. The metaphor of the bridge is an easy image for children of all ages to grasp. Perhaps have your family draw a bridge and then have them place a dot for where they see themselves on the bridge. Do the same thing if you are on a team in an organization experiencing transition.

3. Recognize that this is a heightened season for stress, anxiety and friction. Along the East Coast of the United States, most people know when it's hurricane season. Coastal areas raise flags of warning. People are alert. People tune in to watch developments. How can you be on alert? To expect heightened seasons of stress can help you navigate your new normal.

4. Practice the care of your soul and the care of the souls you love

during this time. For many, moving too quickly will create more potential for stress. Consider these ideas:

- Have a family or team meeting once a week to check in; take the emotional temperature of each family or team member. Ask this question: What's brutal in your world right now? What's beautiful in your world right now?

- Plan a time for a ritual of meaning to take place. Light a candle, use a toy bridge and encourage people to write letters of appreciation to someone who made an impact on their life in the place you've left.

- Use the beautiful wording of Ecclesiastes 3:1-8 and have each person state the season they are in right now and the one they hope to transition to soon.

- Talk and share. Find one person who can listen well if you are the one transitioning, or become the person that someone might need to simply talk to. Make yourself available and have a weekly time where the person can talk about what is happening.

5. Prioritize a list of things that need your attention and sort the list out in the following categories:

- Must be done ASAP

- Can be done within two weeks

- Must give attention to next month

Remember: though everything needs to get done, not everything can or should be done at once. There are priorities of needs. Recognize them.

6. Develop your action plan. We have developed an action plan template for times of transition in the workbook—you may find it helpful. It covers the following topics and more:

- Who do I need to tell my news to and when?

- How can I save my energy for what is really important?

- Who do I need some one-on-one time with and when?

- Who is going to help me move?

- Who am I going to celebrate with?

- Who am I going to grieve with?

- What can I do to help symbolize my time in the season I am now leaving? Who needs to be a part of this special time?

7. Remember lessons learned. Think of ten lessons you learned from this particular stage, phase or season of life. Write them down so you don't forget. Write them down so you can share them with significant people who would benefit from your lessons.

8. Write down your dreams and hopes for the next stage, phase or season of your life. What do you want your next home to be like? What kind of church do you want? What kind of friends do you need right now? What do you want your retirement to look like, feel like and be like—when you actually do retire?

9. Choose a symbol of the past and agree on what that symbol means, then take it with you. In our family we have an ornament for our Christmas tree from every place we've lived and nearly every place we've visited for work or pleasure. Each year, as we decorate the tree, we're reminded through a particular ornament to tell a story, share a memory, laugh or shed another tear. It's our way of honoring our journey. Find your own way to do this.

10. Take your team out for dinner and ask them these questions: What's been the highlight of our work together? What's been the significant takeaway from our time together as team? Don't just leave. When there is no goodbye, everything is unspoken

and unfelt. And that can be deep, dark, and confusing. That is the opposite of leaving well.

All ten of these suggestions are really the work within the work. Each will take time. All will take energy. Most will take imagination. Few of us are good at this because so few of us have been trained to manage our transitions well.

In our most recent staff meeting, I started by asking this question: "What significant things have happened in your life that you want to share with the rest of us?" I was not prepared for what happened next. Every staff member at our ministry revealed a story or situation that revealed they were in major transition. When it was my turn, I chimed in rather innocently, "We have decided to sell our house and move to a home that will need major renovation." Then it hit me. "Oh, my word! I'm in major transition." I need to move slow here and not rush. I need to enjoy the journey and take special care for my wife—who is also going to be in major transition because she is moving with me!

Celtic writer and priest John O'Donohue has written a beautiful book of blessings and prayers titled *To Bless the Space Between Us*. O'Donohue's book can help us in almost every season in life. The words of these blessings give form to the chaos inside. They express for many of us what we simply don't know how to get out. I read one of the blessings to our staff and sensed a joint sigh of exhaustion from all of us. Rebecca had just buried her mom. David had just resigned and was moving on. Craig was about to arrive and begin his work. And on it went. O'Donohue's blessing "For One Who Is Exhausted" offers his blessing and mine to all of us in the weary work we find ourselves in at the present or in the future:

> You have traveled too fast over false ground;
> Now your soul has come to take you back.
> Take refuge in your senses, open up
> To all the small miracles you rushed through.

And he ends the blessing this way:

> Gradually, you will return to yourself,
> Having learned a new respect for your heart
> And the joy that wells far within slow time.[9]

O'Donohue has given us a gift for the work within the work. It is this: When doing the Inside Job, you learn a "new respect for your heart and the joy that wells far within slow time."

Part Three

LEADING TO LIVE

◆

OUR WORK AND OUR LIFE do not have to be lived in silos. We don't have to give attention to one part of our life and neglect the rest. As we journey forward, we can learn to integrate our lives into a whole—into one integrated and connected life. As we do our Inside Job, we address the issues inside that, if left unresolved, will inevitably sideline us—perhaps even disqualify us from embracing the desires and goals we've established.

The final section of the Inside Job addresses the two areas that I explore most with leaders in the marketplace and ministry: resilience and contentment. So here we will explore the necessary ingredients to living a resilient life, and we will conclude the book exploring how to find contentment in life and work. These two issues are important because in most ways in life and work we are looking for the answers of how to keep going strong and how to really be satisfied.

10

LIVING AND LEADING
A RESILIENT LIFE

◆◆◆

Elizabeth Edwards was the wife of US Senator John Edwards of North Carolina. John and Elizabeth Edwards were married for thirty-three years and had four children. John Edwards's career catapulted him into the national news and limelight, and in 2008 he ran unsuccessfully for president of the United States. But what he was successful at was covering up an affair he'd been having with another woman.

Elizabeth was by his side throughout his campaign, working tirelessly for his election. Then she was diagnosed with cancer. John's affair was uncovered and their lives came crashing down. In 2010 he publicly admitted to fathering a child with the other woman. Later that year Elizabeth and John separated. The public rallied around Elizabeth in her fight for life and for recovery from these multiple layers of devastation. In an interview with National Public Radio she said, "Resilience is accepting your new reality, even if it's less good than the one you had before. You can fight it, you can do nothing but scream about what you've lost, or you can accept that and try to put together something that's good." Elizabeth Edwards died of metastatic breast cancer on December 7, 2010, surrounded by family and friends.

When the bottom falls out from under you and you freefall through a divorce or illness or business venture gone south and you emerge from those ashes having put together "something that's good" that's being resilient. Elizabeth Edwards knew that firsthand. So do I.

My Freefall

We moved our family to Colorado to begin a new work—a work I had envisioned where we would come alongside leaders in the marketplace and ministry to offer them soul care. I was offered a great position to begin this venture but it proved to be my undoing—an undoing that offered me a new reality. I was "let go," which means I was fired. The ingredients in that firing were the makings of a great drama. I felt betrayed. I felt abandoned. Most of all, I felt awful.

But within hours of my being fired, friends and family rallied to my side. My brother flew to Colorado to counsel me, and dear friends held us while we wept and lashed out in anger with questions of "How did *this* happen?" In the ashes of that experience, a new way to move on and to move through was birthed in me. My close friends circled and helped me. I spent time alone and time with others. I gave attention to ways I could change and I started to live the life I wanted to live. Now I can say this with clear certainty: Being fired was the best thing that has ever happened to me. I was shaken to the core of my being. I had to reach down deep inside myself and take hold of this new vision. In the crucible of pain and soul-filling agony, my passion was reignited. In Latin, the word for "passion" is connected with the word for "suffering." It was only when I began to suffer that I began to get in touch with what I truly felt I needed to do with my life.

The American humorist Mark Twain said, "The two greatest days of our lives are the day we are born and the day we discover why we were born." In the wake of being fired, I discovered why I was born. All of it resulted in the vision of Potter's Inn as it is today—a ministry devoted to helping marketplace and ministry leaders navigate the whitewaters of life. The pain that undid me was also the pain that saved my life. It taught me to be resilient.

You know by now that we all must do our Inside Job to live a resilient life. A resilient life will not happen unless we do the work within the work. Each of us must figure out what resilience looks like. We all have many things in life that drain us. But what gives us life? What brings us life? Answering these questions is part of the work within the work.

Understanding the Resilient Life

There are at least five components to a resilient life. And there is an ebb and flow to each one:

- a physical life
- an emotional life
- a vocational life
- a relational life
- a stewarding life

You might expect to see "a spiritual life" as one of the components. But the spiritual life is the thread running through all the others. There are no silos in our soul. Everything is connected. We don't build a compartment for the spiritual side of life and put everything in that one place. Rather, our spiritual life moves and expands into all the areas of our life. And our awareness of this grows in time. We wake up to this realization—and sometimes, we wake up later than we might want.

How I treat my body is as much a spiritual matter as whether or not I choose to pray. There is no magical or invisible line that forces a businesswoman to work in the "secular" world while her small group study on Wednesday evenings is "spiritual." God's kingdom covers everything and everyone, so the spiritual sphere of life is all-encompassing.

Let's examine the components of a resilient life and discuss how resilience is fostered, nurtured and cultivated in each one.

A Physical Life

Our physical bodies hold the story of our lives. The wrinkles, scars, birthmarks, frown lines and stress fractures reveal how we have lived. Our bodies are our autobiographies.

Sadly, we have delegated the care of our bodies to the science of medicine and the culture of gyms and workout studios. We have placed our bodies in a silo that says, "What I do with my body is one thing. What I do with my soul is another." This thinking is a lie. Properly understood, our bodies are the address for our souls. Author and philosopher Dallas Willard, quoting French philosopher Pierre Teilhard de Chardin, said it right: "We are spiritual beings having a physical experience."[1] There is a connection between the body and soul that is real and tangible as well as mysterious and evasive.

Resilience has as much to do with the body as it does the soul. We live in our bodies, work in our bodies, make love with our bodies and raise our children in a bodily fashion. If our bodies are tired and worn out, our soul will be also. If we crave sugar, ice cream and quick energy drinks to jolt us up so we can do more, we are displaying a soul problem as well as a physical problem. If we are too anxious and need "something" to help us relax so we can grab every coveted moment of sleep possible, then we have a soul challenge as well as a burgeoning physical dependency on chemicals.

As I write this, I am undergoing a radical paradigm shift in my life. I'm experiencing a "new reality," to use Elizabeth Edwards's words. After almost six decades of living to work, living to eat and living in a stress-filled vocation, I'm now on a journey that is about living to really live. On January 15, 2014, I went to see a medical doctor. I knew something had to be done, and I needed help. So with my doctor's expertise, wisdom and encouragement, coupled with my desire for change, I began. I'm still on this journey toward physical resilience. Perhaps you are too—or you may need to make a decision to do it and do it now. Now—that's the operative word. Don't delay what you know to be important. Now is a really good time to begin.

While I'm no confessed expert and certainly no model, I am on a journey to change the way I live. The first step is to change how I look at food. I had allowed my eating and my body to escape my focus and priority. I was in fact living to eat, meeting with people over lunches, dinners and early morning breakfasts. My intake was a lot more than my output and over the years the pounds increased to an unacceptable, embarrassing and truly humbling level. I felt defeated and hopeless. This was my life, I decided. There was nothing I could do.

But fostering a resilient life begins with looking that lie square in its ugly and contemptuous face and saying, "I need help." I said this to my wife who had nervously and quietly watched me live to eat rather than eat to live. Together we decided to experiment with something she had heard about and was practicing herself. It began with a paradigm shift in my desires. What did I really want? What was I longing for? Digging into these questions provided a foundation I could build on to create a new understanding of nutrition and a renewed commitment to exercise consistently. For me, my paradigm shift was not a diet or a fad program. It was a major overhaul in how I view life, health and my overall well-being.

My paradigm shift began when I realized I needed to get informed about the consequences of my lifestyle and choices and face myself in the mirror. That day I made the conscious choice to live—a choice I encourage you to make with me.

My own awakening involved me realizing what I really want in life:

- I want to see my grandchildren grow up.
- I want to live as independently as possible (having seen both of my parents quest to live independently of my siblings, and many others not able to these days).
- I want to be healthy.
- I want to continue to take long hikes on Colorado pristine trails for as long as I can.
- I want to enjoy this earthly life all the way to the end.

Becoming physically resilient begins with awakening and continues with training. I joined a gym, and it started paying off in a loss of pounds but also in a new feeling inside. I felt alive. I'm convinced that understanding your own desires is the first step toward taking action in any area of life. We have some wonderful exercises and studies on this in the accompanying workbook. Make sure you take the time to work on those as you read this chapter. Take the first step. That's always the hardest one. But that's where resilience begins.

An Emotional Life

Survey the people in your workplace, church, clubs and neighborhoods and I believe you'll find a whole lot of people who struggle with anger, depression and inner turmoil—and that's just the tip of the iceberg. Look a little deeper and you'll find those of us who are bored, stressed out, anxious, phobia-driven and suffering from a host of other "disorders" all working against a resilient emotional life.

Author Peter Scazzero has said it best: "It is impossible to be spiritually mature while remaining emotionally immature."[2] A healthy emotional life is key to living the good life. I know of no other thief robbing people of life more than emotional impoverishment. Men who have not learned to manage their anger, women who have not mastered their lust, CEOs who have not looked at their own dark demons inside, pastors battling rejection, workaholics who leave a trail of carnage behind them in the workplace and church. It's almost overwhelming. We simply cannot be successful on the outside yet feel imprisoned or like victims on the inside and call it a good life.

In chapter two I mentioned that I am presently consulting with a megachurch where the senior pastor was fired and the staff are navigating the whitewater that resulted from this traumatic event. They are disillusioned. In hearing their stories, I've realized the senior pastor was practicing a form of spiritual abuse in neglecting these people under his care. "We're one big dysfunctional family and our senior leader is now the alcoholic," one of them told me. People with dysfunction in their souls lead with dysfunction in their leadership.

What's coming out now is that there were deep emotional wounds in this leader's life. Turns out that this is the third time this leader was fired from church positions across the county. And in this charismatic leader's wake is a new trail of tears from associates whose lives feel wrecked, who feel marginalized and abused. It's sad and terrible what one leader can do when he or she is emotionally unhealthy. A woman on staff shared with me, "He was a tyrant. It was his way or the highway. Now I feel numbed. I can't believe I lived in this toxic environment for ten years."

Living in a toxic environment shaped by an unhealthy leader is deadly. It will maim your own leadership, thwart your own influence, rob you of your joy, diminish your hope and make you feel like nothing more than a cog in the wheel, a widget maker in the machine of church or the corporation. The work environment and culture that is shaped by an unhealthy leader is toxic. There is no sense of thriving, only surviving.

As leaders, we have a responsibility to face the unresolved and unexplored issues in our own lives. We lead in the dark if we don't allow the light to reveal our growth areas. Healthy leadership is viewing ourselves and others with what I call a "3-D" view. By this I mean viewing ourselves and those we lead by seeing not only what is right in front of us but what is inside, around and behind us. This involves getting feedback, gaining perspective and slowing down in our leadership to gain all the necessary perspectives to lead and live well.

Seventy percent of issues that surface during marriage counseling are issues that began prior to the wedding day. This is a staggering statistic. Our emotional wounds start early in life; they're rooted in events that happened to us years ago. Many of these are unresolved issues that have never been examined or reconciled in our minds and hearts. We let these wounds linger and move on through life the best we can. If we're angry, we may not know why our anger flares up and why we can't control it. If we feel ashamed, we may not have examined the genesis of shame in our life and how to get rid of its residue. If we suffer from low self-esteem, perhaps we have we embraced lies about ourselves that breed negative thinking and false realities.

We need to triage our emotional life. "Triage" is a medical word for an assessment of well-being. If you go to an emergency room at a hospital, a nurse will make an assessment of what is going on in you so the healthcare team can make a plan of action to give you help. Attention is given to the most pressing needs first, then the others follow. Looking back at your life and story can reveal the places where the most work needs to be done and done quickly.

A Relational Life

What is truth is this—two are better than one! The Bible says so.

> Two are better than one,
>   because they have a good return for their labor:
> If either of them falls down,
>   one can help the other up.
> But pity anyone who falls
>   and has no one to help them up.
> Also, if two lie down together, they will keep warm.
>   But how can one keep warm alone?
> Though one may be overpowered,
>   two can defend themselves.
> A cord of three strands is not quickly broken. (Ecclesiastes
>   4:9-12 NIV)

The research proves it too:

> Nearly all research into healthy aging has found that the key
> to a long, happy life is not diet or exercise but strong social
> connections—that is, friendships. Loneliness accelerates age-
> related declines in cognition and motor function, while a
> single good friend has been shown to make as much as a 10-
> year difference in overall life expectancy. A huge meta-study
> performed in part at Brigham Young University, which re-
> viewed 148 studies with a combined 308,849 subject partici-
> pants, found that loneliness is just as harmful to health as not
> exercising, smoking 15 cigarettes a day, and alcoholism, and
> fully twice as bad as being obese. Still more startling is a 2010
> study published in the *Journal of Clinical Oncology* that
> looked at 2,230 cancer patients in China. Social well-being,
> including friendship, turned out to be the number one pre-
> dictor of survival.[3]

Relational health is dependent on living our lives in community
with others. Leaders who lead well have others in their lives who

risk sharing the truth—the good and the bad, the positive as well as the negative. These others will also stand in the face of a powerful leader and not be afraid to ask hard questions. We're told in the Bible that we really are our brother's keeper. We keep our sisters' lives also. No one can live life well by living alone. We're not designed to live this way. We were made for community, and in community we live, thrive and make our life count.

I would simply say that if a relationship is not reciprocal—if the other person is not asking you questions, does not explore your own feelings about a subject, and does not invest time, energy or passion back into you—then it's not a healthy friendship. When people are not reciprocal in their interest in you, being with them is work, not relationship. Healthy relationships require a common sharing—an understanding that our friendship is about "we," not just about me. It is your work to figure out who you friends really are—who are the life-giving friends, who breathes life into you when your breath has been knocked out of you?

Social media offers an illusion when it comes to how many friends we have. We can post about our life and have friends "like" what they see. But what about the part of our lives that we don't post? What about the areas of life for which there is no "like" or "favorite" option? What if we are in despair? How does one post about being depressed? When there are no words to describe the grief we feel in the face of profound loss, what can a status update or Tweet offer?

Pseudo-community is the illusion that we're in community with others when we're actually not. Pseudo-community is the appearance that all is well in our world when the opposite is true. True community is built over time and in time. True community involves living out the "one anothers" described in the New Testament. This phrase "one another" appears more than fifty times in the writings of the New Testament. We are to love, encourage, accept, build up, pray for, teach—and many other "one anothers."[4]

Community is built through the ongoing work of depositing love into each other's lives so that when the time for a withdrawal comes, the friendship account is not found to be bankrupt. We make these deposits into each other's souls by caring, showing up, building trust, being safe and loving each other deeply from the heart.

Many professionals today suffer from depletion in their relationships due to the frequency of moves in their careers. Our busyness is another common threat to our relational health. Three friends I know tried to find a night when they could all go out for dinner. It took three weeks for them to find the first available night. This scenario is common even within families today. There seems to be no time to develop meaningful, life-giving relationships, so we become a lone wolf and resign ourselves to surface friendships. We feel alone. We live alone. We do our life alone.

We are designed to live our lives in some form of community. It is not good to be alone—all the time. We need one another to develop meaningful, satisfying and fulfilling lives.

A Vocational Life

The word "vocation" is rooted in the Latin word *vocare*, which means "calling." What are you called to do? What is your life supposed to be about? What, ultimately, do you want to do with your life?

The answers to these questions require a journey. If you hate your work, you might deduce that you hate your life. But if you love your work, you'll experience more of an undivided life—a life that's converged and integrated.[5]

Millions of people play the lottery every week in the hopes of striking it rich and being able to quit work for good. Many think work gets in the way of a fulfilling life. But work actually plays a huge part in our ability to experience a sense of fulfillment and satisfaction.

The problem is what I call "role and soul" confusion. We are unhappy with our work roles and this leads to a confusion about happiness, fulfillment and satisfaction. As we become involved and even obsessed with our work, we can lose touch with our souls. We live divided. We live disintegrated. We live confused.

What we do for a living affects the state of our soul. We spend more time at work than we do at church, for recreation and, for many of us, asleep! Are you connecting the dots here? A toxic work environment is like breathing in toxins into your soul. This results in a poisoned life. It can also result in a toxic leadership style. I've seen this too many times to share here.[6]

A Stewarding Life

We came into this world with nothing and we will leave this world with nothing. There is nothing that we own, nothing that we have acquired and nothing that we'll get next year that we can take with us when we die. Given this reality, we have an important role to live out, and that is the role of being a steward. Stewardship, when best understood, is simply the act of managing one's life well—all of one's life: resources, talents, time and treasures.

Stewardship is about giving back. We can change the name to anything we like—"pay it forward," "philanthropy" or "mission"— but at the core of any act of stewardship is the giving of our time, resources and abilities. As we give, something happens inside us. We sense that we are part of something greater than ourselves. We realize we are giving some part of ourselves.

The fruit of the Spirit is not hoarding, holding on to, or stashing away one's resources. As we live, we learn to give. It's an important lesson that the apostle Paul wrote about many times in his letters to the new followers of Jesus' movement:

I've never, as you so well know, had any taste for wealth or fashion. With these bare hands I took care of my own basic needs and those who worked with me. In everything I've done, I have demonstrated to you how necessary it is to work on behalf of the weak and not exploit them. You'll not likely go wrong here if you keep remembering that our Master said, "You're far happier giving than getting." (Acts 20:33-35)

Every day we make choices that are grounded in our belief about stewarding our life well. We choose to share, to leave our work on time, to invest our lives in what really matters in life. As author Annie Dillard has said, "How you live your days is how you will live your life." You don't get the chance at the end of your life to choose how you want to be remembered. You are making that choice each and every day right now. The choice to steward life well begins with smaller choices of what you will do each day with your time, talents and treasures. Let me explain.

If you want to be remembered as a "sharing" or "giving" person, then that will depend on how you share your time and resources today. Did you notice the needy today? Did you take the time to go out of your way to *be* the answer to a need in someone's life?

Stewarding our resources is something the Bible speaks about from beginning to end. Since we were created in the image of a benevolent, loving and giving God, we too must give. If our work has captured all our time, all our energy, and all our passion, then we will need to reassess this reality in light of our desire to be become better stewards of our money, resources and time. Managing our time so that we have some time to give away requires us to marshal our energies wisely. It's one of the apostle Peter's eight virtues, remember? Being a steward requires that we grow into becoming people who have "self-control." We will not spend everything we have. We will not choose to invest only in our work. We will choose to invest in others, including those who have true need.

When travelling recently I stopped at a coffee shop in Cape Town, South Africa. The waiter came up with a huge smile on his face and cracked a joke. I liked him immediately. He seemed different. I asked, "How long have you worked in this coffee shop?"

"Ten years," he replied.

"Are you married?"

"Yes."

"Do you have children?"

"Yes, two, ages three and six."

I probed further. "Do you want to spend the rest of your life working here?"

"Of course not. I want to be a tour guide. I want to show people like you my beautiful country."

I found out through my own tour guide that a person could take a course and graduate as a licensed tour guide for four hundred dollars. I decided right then and there to invest in JR. For an investment of four hundred dollars, I could help steward someone's life to a better place. We could have spent that money on gifts, souvenirs or a game drive to see wild animals. But when I was faced with the opportunity to participate in someone's vocational breakthrough, it was a no-brainer.

I was able to set up a way to pay for JR's training. He's now doing what he really wanted to do but could not find a way to do. I partnered with my own tour guide to make sure things were set up and asked him to act as a mentor and friend to JR.

I wish I could tell you that's been my style of stewarding for all my life. But in reality, I have had to grow in my own understanding of what it means to steward my life and resources well. Giving has been cultivated in me over the years. But it began with a choice and a commitment to be a steward and not a hoarder of my time, talents and treasures.

The work that I do, the calling that I fulfill and the influence that

God has given me have all resulted from men and women who have believed in me, invested their resources in me and stewarded their own money toward me. If it were not for the generous stewardship of marketplace leaders there would be no book, no retreat center, no ministry. The principle of stewardship expands one's influence beyond your own reach. The people who invest in my work invest because they believe in me, have built trust with me and have seen the fruit of their investment, which brings them a deep satisfaction. I am the humble recipient of women and men who live this out every single day and if you are benefiting from this book, then you too are a part of their stewarding life.

Let's review. I've been exploring five areas of our lives:

- a physical life
- an emotional life
- a vocational life
- a relational life
- a stewarding life

In looking at this list, where do you feel you need the most work? Can you see that each of these areas is part of your spiritual life? Your spiritual life is more than having a quiet time then going on to do your work. Your spiritual life is the integration of all that makes you you!

In thinking through my own life, I have found that from time to time, one of these areas gets neglected, overlooked or forgotten. As a result of neglecting one area, the other areas seem to suffer. My health simply cannot pay the price for success in another area. I'm not good if my work schedule has caused me to be stressed out with no time for friends, resulting in high blood pressure and gaining weight. The key is to look at these areas as integrated—each one important to the whole life you are living, each one vital to a resilient life.

Which one of these five aspects of your own life seems most in need of your time and attention? Decide and get started. Make a plan. Use the online resources that we have for you at www.my insidejob.com. The best scenario is this: enlist another person— perhaps three or four others who you want to invest in their own well-being—and get started.

The Work of Rest

To live a resilient life, we need to rest—something crucial to living not only a good life, but a life of receiving what only rest can offer us. As we've already discussed earlier, most Americans do not take all their allotted vacation time. Is it out of fear that someone else might replace them while they're gone? Is rest overrated? Do we even know how to rest? Many people I work with explain their vacations based on activity: the times of skiing in Colorado, swimming and scuba diving in the ocean of Africa, tennis at the club. But tours, sightseeing and fast-moving regimens are perhaps not the best way to experience the rest our souls are calling out for.

Have you wondered sometimes why you're so tired after a vacation? But wait a moment; what did you do on that vacation? How much energy did you expend on mountain climbing, surfing or kayaking? How many nights were you "out" rather than away? How much sleep did you actually get doing all of that fun stuff? If you're exhausted from your vacation, then it's time to learn how to take a real rest.

Our culture is in need of learning this most basic skill. As Peter has reminded us, we've left what we used to know and found ourselves at a dangerous dead end. One of the things we need to learn is how to rest and live within our limits. Author and poet David Whyte opens our minds and hearts to rest when he writes:

Rest is the conversation between what we love to do and how

we love to be. Rest is the essence of giving and receiving. Rest is an act of remembering, imaginatively and intellectually but also physiologically and physically. To rest is to give up on the already exhausted will as the prime motivator of endeavor, with its endless outward need to reward itself through established goals. To rest is to give up on worrying and fretting and the sense that there is something wrong with the world unless we put it right; to rest is to fall back literally or figuratively from outer targets and shift the goal not to an inner bulls eye, an imagined state of perfect stillness, but to an inner state of natural exchange.[7]

This kind of rest does not come naturally for us in a wired world with busyness everywhere on the outside and stress within us. Here are some guidelines that many have found helpful in learning how to rest. Let's look at the stages of rest—and then practice them.

The first stage of rest: stop. Before you rest, you must first stop. Stop doing and start being. After all, we're not human doings, we're human beings. If you allow your voicemail, texting and email to go with you on your time off, you're not having time off. You are still on. Disengage from all forms of technology. Stop the email. Stop the texting. Stop the voicemail. Put everything on "stop." Set up an auto-reply or, better, unplug. By unplugging, you say to yourself and to others, "I am now detached. I am now truly unavailable to others. I am intentionally choosing to be available to myself, my heart and my soul and perhaps the few I love who are with me." If you are exhausted, be exhausted. Enter the exhaustion and don't force yourself to do anything. Sleep. Nap. Trickle-charge.

The second stage of rest: slow down. Practice slowing down as an art form. For one thing, don't start reading anything. Why? Because you need a bit of transition time to let the swirling wind settle within and without. Besides, you most likely cannot take anything in right now. Be kind to yourself. Eat slow. Move slow. Practice Dallas Willard's oft-quoted secret of the spiritual life: "Ruthlessly eradicate hurry from your life." This of course is countercultural—really, it's a prophetic call to live life differently right now.

Let slow be the new normal. While speed and hurry is the normal back home, now nothing is screaming at you except your body's care, your soul's care and your mind's care. To repair all of the damage done inside and outside you, you must truly slow down.

The third stage of rest: arrival. In the death and burial of Jesus, by the third day there was resurrection. If you've truly stopped, if you've slowed down, then the long-awaited, hoped-for and primal truth of your own resurrection is right around the corner. Trust the process. Give yourself two to three days of slowing and doing nothing before you do anything. By the third day of your time away or your vacation you can read a book, play games, ride a bike and go dancing. Ask yourself, "What would give me life today?" Then go and do just that! Do nothing that will not bring you life. Now you're more alive and more awake! You can stay up late and watch a movie without falling asleep. While awake, you can notice the beauty and take the beauty into that place in you where it will do its healing work.

The fourth stage of rest: play. This is the indulgence of that simple urge to enjoy, laugh and bask. It is truly recreation. We re-create the loss of time and space in our lives. We find each other through games and doing those things that are life-giving.

Virginia Postrel, a leading social commentator, writes, "Play nurtures a supple mind, a willingness to think in new categories, and an ability to make unexpected associations. . . . The spirit of play not only encourages problem solving but, through novel analogies, fosters originality and clarity."[8]

"Nothing lights up the brain like play," says researcher Stuart Brown.[9] If you feel as if you're lost and living in a dark space, play could be part of the light you need to find your way back. Remember, we're told in the Bible to call the Sabbath—a day of rest—a pleasure. Pleasure breeds more pleasure—not dread, not fear, not anxiety, but this beautiful word that is more than a word: an actual experience of pleasure.

You enjoy sitting in the sun; you find yourself finally able to laugh again and know that laughing is good. And you bask—that ancient art of lingering, soaking in and marinating to absorb everything and everyone to the very last drop.

The fifth stage of rest: remember. Did you know that in the Ten Commandments, the only commandment we are told to "remember" is the Sabbath. Why is this? Most likely because God knew we would quickly forget to rest. We get an A in living by the sweat of our brow. But we don't get high marks for resting and ceasing. When we remember our time off, we savor the time and we laugh at the crazy things that happened. We recall the good food. We remember the feelings that surged up within us when we saw the mountain vista or sunset at the shore. Remembering is about storytelling, and in every story of how we rested and enjoyed time and life, the soul finds comfort.

Finally, we can anticipate our own reentry to the life we've left. But what we just experienced on our respite was real. We make a horrible and tragic mistake when we say only work is real. This is not the truth. Rest is real and until we rest, we run our lives on empty. Rest is the God-given, God-ordained and God-modeled way to truly live.

As we journey through our work and life, our reality will change several times. We will change jobs. We will change where we live. Our children will grow up and leave the nest. Our spouse may die.

When our children were small, my wife drove a big, old and very well-used Suburban we nicknamed "the Grizzly." It was built for the outdoors—four-wheel drive, steel plates underneath to protect the chasse from stumps and boulders, and built for endurance. The great thing about the Grizzly was that it was big and wide. It would haul our kids, plus all of our gear for mountain camping. However, the problem with the Grizzly was also that it was big and wide. Gwen, my wife and primary driver of the Grizzly, developed a reputation for knocking down mailboxes and road signs and taking out shrubs and trees in the neighborhood. When I talked to Gwen about these issues, she lamented, "Steve, the Grizzly is so big and has so many blind spots I feel as if I'm driving a tank. Get me a smaller car or you'll have to deal with all my blind spots." We got another smaller car for her and she quit knocking over others' personal property.

Blind spots are an issue not only in driving but in life as well. Sometimes we just can't see the reality of what's about to happen. We're blind to it. As we move through life, we may find that a key area that helps foster a resilient life is missing. The reason? We're blind to it. Our work may be going well, but what about our health? How are we handling all the stress? We may be getting awards and bonuses but do we have good friends to share in the joy with us? Blind spots are easy to ignore because of the speed with which we move through life. We may resign ourselves to think, "Well, this is just the way it is. There's nothing I can do about it. Everyone has something going on inside—this is just my issue."

We can try to justify blind spots. We can deny they're real. We can ignore them. But here's the truth: Blind spots have a way of rearing up and becoming larger than life and can result in massive damage that is far, far more extensive than mowing down a few mailboxes or taking out a half-dozen azalea bushes. Blind spots in health will kill us as stress rises and blood pressure goes unchecked. Blind spots in relationships will sever blood ties and cause massive wounds in the family.

It is our Inside Job to do a 360-degree walk around our own life, with the help of a friend to help us really see what we cannot. No one can live a resilient life without giving attention to both potential blind spots and to each of the five areas we've surveyed in this chapter.

11

Leading with Contentment and Satisfaction

◆

I hope what you have seen so far in this book is this: There is a better way to live. There is an alternative to the craziness. There are preventive measures, work that if done now will help us escape the tragedies we read and hear about among our leaders today. You will have to agree that:

- I don't have to live this way.
- I don't need to lead the way we've led in the past.
- The better way to live and lead is to follow the ways of Jesus.
- I must do my Inside Job by accessing my situation and embracing the changes that need to be made.
- I must choose to be a part of the solution to the crisis by living well and leading well. Everything begins with me. I can't lead change unless I change.
- I must develop the eight virtues by choosing to live the right way and do the right thing each and every day.
- I must take a hard look at my dark side within. I must lead from the light, not from the dark.

- I must choose to live in rhythm by taking the required time to detox, enjoy the peace of solitude and quiet, and practice my own Sabbath.

- I must accept my limits and relinquish the lie that I can do everything and anything I want to do.

- By managing my own transitions better, I will care for myself better and live better with those around me.

- Everything I do in my Inside Job will help me live a life that is resilient—a life I actually want to live.

Not Only You

And while it is up to you, it is also not up to you. That's the paradox of our transformation; it does not depend solely on us. Authentic transformation depends on the "divine power" that Peter says "has given us everything we need for a godly life" (2 Peter 1:3 NIV). The Bible is clear. God is at work within us. We are assured of this fact. God is at work in our own work within the work. This work is really a passion God has for all of us—that we grow, change and become better versions of ourselves. Paul reminds us:

> What I'm getting at, friends, is that you should simply keep on doing what you've done from the beginning. When I was living among you, you lived in responsive obedience. Now that I'm separated from you, keep it up. Better yet, redouble your efforts. Be energetic in your life of salvation, reverent and sensitive before God. That energy is *God's* energy, an energy deep within you, God himself willing and working at what will give him the most pleasure. (Philippians 2:12-13)

This Inside Job happens because God is at work to help shape us into becoming the better version of ourselves. His energy becomes our energy. Our energy alone is suspect and is at best insufficient to bring about our own transformation. I say "suspect" because the Inside Job is far, far more than self-help. It is God who wants our transformation even when we'd prefer to stay stuck in our addictions and remain in our tombs even though we sense that there is life right outside if we'd only move forward. We have something more. We have Someone. The God we sing to, the God we praise, the God we say we live for is with us at every point in our journey.

Visible or invisible, God meets us along the way and infuses us with his great help. Bidden or unbidden, God is here. We can take this help to the bank and make many, many deposits into our souls. This help and God's presence in our lives happen in practical and mysterious ways. The practical ways are easier to comprehend. The mysterious ways are more complicated. We live in a bigger story than just working until we retire. God is working in us—and this single fact sets us up for a glorious adventure. These ways involve God's Spirit working change in us from the inside out. We learn that in ways we cannot see or quantify. We partner with him in our own transformation as we practice these new ways and incorporate them into our lives.[1] There is no secular work. There is no work that God is not involved in, no matter your vocation. God's vocation is clear. God seeks to shape us all into better versions of ourselves—better clay pots without the marrings we have explored in this book.

There is a better way to live and lead. There is a way that fosters peace within, a way that grows contentment and satisfaction. This way will mess with you until you get your life straightened out and are living the life you long to live. I say "mess with you" because once you learn about living in rhythm and then begin to actually do it, you'll wonder why you never did so before. When you accept your limits and manage transitions well, you will not be so breathless during the changes that come your way and redefine life ahead. You'll lay down competing ambitions and embrace the life you've been given.

Once you taste a little resilience, you will not go back to trying to do more and more to find what "more" will never offer you. You'll still make mistakes and make decisions that were not in your best interest or those of others around you, but you'll be learning from them instead of blindly agreeing to repeat them in the future. The Inside Job is allowing our friends and colleagues, the birds and flowers, our pastors, spiritual mentors and wise sages to become our companions. I've always loved the words of Martin Luther, the sixteenth-century reformer of the church gone wrong, in his commentary on Jesus' words when he told us to consider the flowers and look at the birds (Matthew 6:26-29). Luther said, "Sometimes, birds should become our teachers and flowers, our theologians." More than ever in my life than right now, I am finally understanding Luther's wisdom! He is speaking about the lessons we learn in silence and solitude as we do our Inside Job.

Can't Get No Satisfaction

What it boils down to is this: We long for satisfaction in life. We watch the ads on TV and see people living a life we want but can't seem to find. Nearly all our efforts and all our yearnings are rooted in our search for satisfaction. Peter, along with all the early followers of Jesus, were in the same hunt we are today. When Peter fished all day and night and caught nothing, we can fully understand his stress. Satisfaction then for Peter was a full net of fish. But as Peter followed Jesus and practiced his ways of life and in leadership, satisfaction morphed into contentment.

Nothing has really changed with us and our pursuits in life. Then as now our goal is not a feeling of satisfaction but rather to be captured by a contentment that takes root in the heart and blossoms around us. It is as if we cast a mood of contentment to those we are doing life with, to our colleagues and to the people we most love. Contentment grows and oozes over into the lives of others. Living this way is true mission, and I believe it is our great commission to first live at peace with ourselves and others and then to let others see the transformation in us. Our transformed lives will result in people being thirsty for what we've found that quenches our soulful thirst—a thirst that money will not buy and wealth will not satisfy.

Isaiah, a Jewish prophet who lived and worked eight hundred years before Jesus' birth, understood the thirst and the alternative ways we seek to gain satisfaction:

> Hey there! All who are thirsty,
> > come to the water!
> Are you penniless?
> > Come anyway—buy and eat!
> Come, buy your drinks, buy wine and milk.
> > Buy without money—everything's free!
> Why do you spend your money on junk food,
> > your hard-earned cash on cotton candy?
> Listen to me, listen well: Eat only the best,
> > fill yourself with only the finest.
> Pay attention, come close now,
> > listen carefully to my life-giving, life-nourishing words.
> > > (Isaiah 55:1-3)

Don't speed-read that! Go back and read it slowly and let the words stick like Velcro to your heart. Friends, we have not eaten the best there is when we are living the American way over the way of Jesus.

I'll never forget watching a documentary titled *Happiness*. The documentary shows several families all over the world in various social stations of life all seeking happiness. As it turns out, the happiest folks are among those who have the least in life—not the most.

Their contentment is within. My fellow pilgrims, the journey to gain your own contentment is within your own heart, not in a new house or office space. It's that simple.

In an earlier chapter, I made a distinction between outer and inner markers of success. Far too much of our success these days is determined by outer markers—money, the neighborhood we live in, what we drive and so on. Satisfaction depends on these outer trappings, and like those trappings it is fleeting at best and (eventually) boring at worst. Much of satisfaction is driven by us. We're satisfied when *we* have met a goal. We're satisfied when *we* have accomplished something. We're satisfied when *we* have met someone who meets our needs. But contentment, while not oblivious to outer markers, is not defined by them.

When I went to my medical doctor for my physical, he asked me a question no doctor had ever asked me. "Steve, how do you define 'life'?" He was examining more than my pulse and the oxygen level in my blood. He wanted me to articulate something much deeper. He said, "I'll give you until your next appointment to answer it. But write down what you think life is—or even should be—and bring it with you next time." I agreed.

If you try to answer this question, I think you'll find, like me, that outer markers of success will not inform your answer. You will look for something more—something deeper.

When I ask that question to folks who come see me for the care of their soul, I rarely hear anyone say, "Life is about success." Or "Life is having more power, position and prestige." People answer this question with words describing contentment and peace.

Contentment is deep, stable, unswayed by circumstances and unimpressed by the swaggers of our day. Since childhood most of us have been searching for approval—to be accepted, to receive applause and praise. As adults many of us are still doing the same today. Due to the shaping force of culture and the absent voices of prophets who could set the record straight and tell us how it really is, we believe that happiness and satisfaction come from money, sex, power, prestige, position and success. Not only some money and some success, but more—more of everything. Since there is never enough of what we seek, we pedal faster and spin on the hamster wheel longer until we're sure the pot of gold that has always eluded is just within our grasp. Then we wake up to empty, senseless lives that have no purpose or meaning. Unhappiness and discontentment is really a dis-ease that is epidemic today. We are sick from the way we live and lead. We sow the wind and reap the whirlwind, as another prophet warned us.

Has it ever occurred to you to become suspicious of the ways people are trying to experience happiness and satisfaction? How did these lies and standards get so programmed into our thinking?

We have no one to blame but ourselves. The invention of the light bulb, the Industrial Revolution, the 24/7 way we live today—always being "on" and always being available—have contributed. All of us have helped shape this broken culture we survive in today. We have put our own shoulder to the plow and reaped what the seeds planted in our hearts can never give us. We think happiness will come in the reaping. Happiness will be one day soon. Payday is coming—that will be happiness. Happiness will come when we manage our lives better and finally give up and quit and have enough to live on for the rest of our lives. Happiness seems always to be in the future.

But contentment is learned. We learn on the journey that contentment is manifested within us. It is an attitude and posture that comes as we live in the way, walk in the way and lead in the way.

Being content is the by-product of doing the Inside Job. As we do the work within the work, we foster contentment. We give contentment the space and place it needs to take root and grow. This is the key. This is the secret that is really not a secret after all. It's been there for us all along. It's just that we've been duped and fooled into drinking the other stuff.

Contentment is the result of being honest with ourselves and others around us. We strike water in the well of contentment when we read Isaiah's words again and again at intervals along our journey and confess: "The water I've been drinking is not really water at all. It's got a long list of ingredients in it that someone somewhere along the way led me to believe I needed to quench my thirst." When you are honest with who you are and what your opinions are and decide that you really do believe what you say you believe, then you honor this acceptance of not only your beliefs but yourself—the true you!

In choosing to be the true you—to be your true self—you lay down your efforts to prove something—that you are lovable, that you are gifted, that you are worth something. When you accept yourself, there is tremendous peace that arises within the soul. To be honest with yourself means you will exert the courage to be yourself and quit trying to be someone else. You choose to live and lead from the core of who you are—a core that has its foundation in the eight virtues of 2 Peter 1.

Contentment is not based on our efforts. We don't have to *do* something *more* to be content. Actually, we may find that growing in contentment leads us to do less, and that realization may in fact lead us to quit trying so hard. We learn to let go and quit clutching everything and everyone so tightly. We relax and loosen our grip—give up our need to control, to push our ideas at every meeting, to share the wisdom we have accumulated on certain topics and to express our opinions on everything from politics to theology to the latest get-rich scheme.

Contentment flows into us and out of us. There is something about being content that is a spiritual reality—a reality God wants for his children. I believe God wants us to experience this contentment just as I want my own children to live in peace with their spouses, with their own children, in their communities and with those they call church—the called-out ones who follow the ways of Jesus.

Perhaps now we are ready to hear what Paul, the contemporary and teammate of Peter, said about learning to be content. He wrote what we are about to read while chained in a prison cell—not exactly an outer marker of success, wouldn't you agree? Paul writes:

> I am not saying this because I am in need, for I have learned to be content whatever the circumstances. I know what it is to be in need, and I know what it is to have plenty. I have learned the secret of being content in any and every situation, whether well fed or hungry, whether living in plenty or in want. I can do all this through him who gives me strength. (Philippians 4:11-13 NIV)

Contentment is a posture that we learn in life. We learn this lesson in hard and challenging times when perhaps some of our idols have come crashing down to our feet, revealing their powerlessness once and for all. We learn in the simple moments in life what makes us feel alive and what makes us feel dead. We put two and two together somewhere along the journey and say, "I've got it now. I've learned something really important. I know where the well is and I will only drink from *this* well." Contentment involves our well-being—a well-being that is clearly marked with the inner markers that we have discussed in this book.

Shalom Life

Shalom is the great Hebrew word for what has come to be known in the English language as "peace." But as we discussed in chapter seven, that simple translation is deficient. The deeper meaning of the word reveals something significant for us in our pursuit of living well. A life of shalom is a life of completeness, wholeness, health, peace, welfare, safety, soundness, tranquility, serenity and fullness. It is a life absent of discord, unhappiness and restlessness. That's the actual definition of the word.

Where do we sign up for that? Where can we get a life of shalom? Shalom is not only what I most deeply long for in my own life but it is what I most want for my children and grandchildren. Stop and ask yourself, "What do I really want in life?" At some point in your answer, I believe you will articulate the longing of your soul and every soul—to live a shalom life. I want a shalom marriage. I want a shalom work environment. I want my teammates to have a life of shalom as well. I want to go to a shalom church. I want to be involved in organizations that seek to bless others with the shalom of God—a shalom we cannot muster, a shalom we did not invent and cannot patent. This shalom energy is from another world—a place where God dwells, a place where I will spend eternity.

A life of shalom is a life blessed by inner security and outer peace. Shalom comes from within. It is not attached or added on like a Christmas tree ornament. A life of shalom is nurtured and developed through all the stages and phases of our lives.

Our well-being is at stake. We have to distinguish between what we want and what we need to live in shalom. And the simple truth is that we don't really need a lot. But we do need to give attention to all the factors that contribute to our well-being: our health, our relationships, our work, our family and our emotional health.

In giving attention to each one of these areas, I am fostering a life of shalom. When I feel deficient in one of these areas, I don't run my soul into the ground, live my life on empty and simply press on with a prayer that I will someday become happy. No, I do the Inside Job. I do it every single day. I live with great intentionality, because if I only hope that the shalom life will come to me like a lottery windfall one day, then I am delusional.

Like you, I am learning more about this process in each new step of my own journey. I have a wise spiritual director with whom I process my own journey each month. I talk. I open my heart and say how life really is. And then we dig into the mess together and sort through what is true and what is an illusion. I experience shalom each time I do this because I am reminded of what I must be reminded of:

I am loved.

I am blessed.

I am forgiven.

I am not alone.

St. Ireneaus once said, "The glory of God is a man fully alive." The Inside Job is your wake-up call to live before you die. Your death is certain. I promise you that! But some people die before they ever live. May this not be the case with you. The Inside Job is your manual to live well in the shalom sense—not as my friend tells me is living well, not as the world tells me is living well. A life of shalom is a life radiating of true blessing anchored in a person's soul and shining outward to others around them.

Contentment Is Within

Let me explain this with a modern-day parable I have heard told by others: the story of the Mexican fisherman and the banker.

An American investment banker was taking a much-needed vacation in a small coastal Mexican village when a small boat carrying one fisherman docked. The boat held several large fresh fish.

The investment banker was impressed by the quality of the fish and asked the Mexican how long it took to catch them. The Mexican replied, "Only a little while." The banker asked why the fisherman hadn't stayed out longer and caught more fish.

The Mexican fisherman replied that he had enough to support his family's immediate needs.

The American asked, "But what do you do with the rest of your time?"

The Mexican fisherman replied, "I sleep late, fish a little, play with my children, take siesta with my wife, stroll into the village, sip wine and play guitar with my amigos. I have a full and busy life, señor."

The investment banker scoffed. "I am an Ivy League MBA, and I could help you. You could spend more time fishing and with the proceeds buy a bigger boat, and with the proceeds from the bigger boat you could buy several boats until eventually you would have a whole fleet of fishing boats. Instead of selling your catch to the middleman you could sell directly to the processor, eventually opening your own cannery. You could control the product, processing and distribution."

Then he added, "Of course, you would need to leave this small coastal fishing village and move to Mexico City where you would run your growing enterprise."

The Mexican fisherman asked, "But señor, how long will this all take?"

The American replied, "Fifteen to twenty years."

"But what then?" asked the Mexican.

The American laughed and said, "That's the best part. When the time is right you announce an IPO and sell your company stock to the public and become very rich. You make millions."

"Millions, señor? Then what?"

The investment banker said, "Then you would retire. You could move to a small coastal fishing village where you would sleep late, fish a little, play with your kids, take siesta with your wife, stroll to the village in the evenings, sip wine and play your guitar with your amigos."

As good stories do, this tale makes us laugh and cry at the same time. But it also reveals an important point that every leader needs to realize: Contentment is within us, not outside us.

Once more, take Peter as an example. Peter was imprisoned but was found in his prison cell singing songs, not crying (see Acts 12). He was content. And his contentment was not due to outer things, such as the ambiance or lack thereof in his prison cell. Peter's contentment was within.

Peter knew that silver and gold were not the basis of contentment. When he was an emerging leader in the early movement of the explosion of the faith, he encountered a handicapped man begging (see Acts 3). Peter was not a wealthy small business owner at this time. He had laid aside his fishing nets and taken on new work—the work of guiding the movement Jesus started. When the beggar kept calling out for Peter to give him some money, Peter stated confidently:

> "I don't have a nickel to my name, but what I do have, I give you: In the name of Jesus Christ of Nazareth, walk!" He grabbed him by the right hand and pulled him up. In an instant his feet and ankles became firm. He jumped to his feet and walked. (Acts 3:6-8)

Peter's confidence was not in the power of money. It was in the power of God. This was a lesson he learned in the years he apprenticed with Jesus, when he heard Jesus' teachings on contentment, the power of money and the false allure of positions.[2]

I imagine that Peter had heard his colleague Paul speak on the source of contentment many times. They were coworkers and contemporaries and shared the same journey of doing the Inside Job. Paul's story of doing the work within the work is an incredible account of someone who had power, position and security yet realized the black hole of it all when he encountered the way of Jesus. Paul was also in a prison cell. It was from this prison that he wrote to the church about contentment and happiness:

> I don't have a sense of needing anything personally. I've

learned by now to be quite content whatever my circumstances. I'm just as happy with little as with much, with much
as with little. I've found the recipe for being happy whether
full or hungry, hands full or hands empty. Whatever I have,
wherever I am, I can make it through anything in the One
who makes me who I am. (Philippians 4:11-13)

The recipe that Paul describes and that Peter lived is this:

1) Choose to view life and work from a wider perspective than
that of your circumstances. You may not be in the place or job you
want, but what's the hurry? Learn the lessons your circumstances
offer you now so you can use them later. Paul was in prison. But his
heart was not in prison. He gave thanks in all things because a
wider and higher perspective helped him see a bigger picture and
larger story.

2) We can rest in our circumstances because God is ultimately in
control and we are not. After a terrible accident left the missionary
Amy Carmichael paralyzed, she wrote, "In acceptance, there is great
peace." There may be nothing you can really do about your circumstances. Sometimes we must lay down our efforts to change something outside us and change our internal perspective instead.

3) Contentment grows as we do our part and God does his. It
grows as we do our Inside Job and God does the work within that
only he can do. He gives peace. We can't acquire it any other way.
But by choosing to live in rhythm, we sow the seeds of peace in our
lives that only a Sabbath rest can give. We participate in our own
transformation by practicing healthy and holy habits that foster
more peace than we have when we do things our own way.

4) As we rise above our circumstances, we rise to a higher plane
of living. Life is more than "what happens to us when making plans."
Life is not our accumulated circumstances that may contain layoffs,
economic downturns and illness. Life is a sacred gift to be stew-

arded well. Our individual stories of work, life and faith have varied circumstances that distinguish one story, one life from another, but the great themes for all of us are redemption, struggle, perseverance and freedom. All of the great stories recorded in the Bible are anchored in these great themes. Circumstances do not define us. What defines us as human beings is our Inside Job. My dog, Laz, a beautiful seven-year-old golden retriever, has no Inside Job to do. No thought ever crosses his mind about work that needs to be done other than to be loved and to love me back. We as humans, however, have the task of the Inside Job.

5) Remember, life doesn't revolve around us. We foster contentment as we help others live well—we serve and give. We live and help others live. As we love others, the greatest paradox of our lives happens within us—we are loved back.

The Inside Job

The Inside Job is about learning to live for what is really important, for what truly matters. Our culture presents some interesting options for our consideration these days. But my hope here has been to help you think through some better options and to do your own work. The real work for you is about becoming the person you were created to be, a better version of yourself. It is about working on the dark sides—the addictions and lies we have acquired and believed along the way. As we follow the way, we jettison the things we no longer need, things we're tempted to hold on to, things we have falsely believed will make us happy. The Inside Job is the work we do to live in the true blessing that comes our way as we change, grow and mature.

Our Inside Job is about awakening. It seems like Jesus was always telling his early followers to "wake up." They fell asleep at the most awkward moments and didn't pay close attention to many of Jesus' revolutionary teachings. We can also cruise along the way with

Jesus. We may need to wake up from a long, sleepy, lulled life. When we wake up and get out of our stupor, we realize that we really don't have to live or lead in a crazy way. We are jarred into turning our lives around, and as we do, we live well and lead well.

Jesus had much to say on this subject. And as we awaken to new realities that have been long ignored or perhaps forgotten, I hope the words of Jesus will come to mean as much to you as they do for me. Among Jesus' many opportunities to help us comprehend what he was both living and describing, he said this: "What good will it be for someone to gain the whole world, yet forfeit their soul?" (Matthew 16:26 NIV). Somewhere along the way as we wake up, we must ask ourselves this question: What do I lose through all of my gaining, and is it worth it?

Peter's voice calls us to the truth that can set us free—to the truth of what is right, tried, tested and relevant for all people. We can thank Peter for his voice today—and we should. Peter paid a great price to live with such moral courage and spiritual conviction. No one is really sure how Peter's life ended, but legend tells us that he was crucified upside down—thinking he was not worthy for his life to end the same way as that of his mentor in life, teacher in truth and real Savior from his darkened ways.

A Light in Dark Times

We have a light in dark times. We are not left alone. This same light that illuminated Peter's way will do the same for us. Peter starts his letter to us by sincerely stating, "Grace and peace be yours in abundance" (2 Peter 1:2 NIV). Our Inside Job is to maintain that grace and peace "in abundance" in our work as well as in our lives. This is key to understanding what Jesus meant when he described that the life of his followers would be a "rich and satisfying life" (John 10:10). The word is "abundant life" in other translations. This is a life wedded with peace, contentment and happiness.

I began this book with the parable of the wood carver. I want to conclude with another parable, this one just as simple to understand and just as crucial for doing the Inside Job:

> A group of tourists sit in a bus that is passing through gorgeously beautiful country; lakes and mountains and green fields and rivers. But the shades of the bus are pulled down. They do not have the slightest idea of what lies beyond the windows of the bus. And all the time of their journey is spent in squabbling over who will have the seat of honor in the bus, who will be applauded, who will be well considered. And so they remain till the journey's end.[3]

Don't miss the gorgeous, beautiful country. The good life is waiting for you. It's going to take work. But you can do it.

Acknowledgments

◆◆◆

M any voices (far too many to list here) have contributed to my own Inside Job—a work I have been giving attention to for more than sixty years now. Every place I have worked, I have realized that men and women have sought to work on me to be a better leader, a better man, a better husband, a better father, a better friend. I am grateful for each person who sought to sharpen and help me and thus hopefully help you, the reader.

Inside Job is the fruit of my work with leaders whose lives have become the fodder for the fire of transformation. Their stories have all informed the insights, lessons and principles I share here. I am thankful for each story and each life that has informed my own life of how utterly crucial it is for each of us to do our Inside Job.

In the writing of this book, my editor John Blase helped sharpen the focus and improve the paragraphs. He believed in me in this book, and I am very grateful. Caleb Seeling helped guide me well in the early days of this book's pilgrimage to be birthed into the book you hold here. Thank you!

The wonderful folks at InterVarsity Press embraced this book and message and have now championed it. I am particularly grateful for Cindy Bunch's expertise and belief in me. Jeff Crosby so believed in this book that he flew out to our retreat and shared the story of his own Inside Job. There and then we became fast friends and allies. A special thank you goes to the entire team at IVP. I'm honored to have this book in the long line of thoughtful books you publish.

The team that works with me at Potter's Inn lives this message out with me in their own work with leaders who come to our retreat center week after week. Dustin and Natalie Hibbard, Craig and Karen Hamlow, Charles and Linda Snow and Rebecca Eims Hinebaugh are my allies, companions, friends and skilled laborers in the hearts of many. Thank you for your work with me.

Each of the endorsers of this book, I owe my deepest thanks. You have stood with me, coached me, cheered me and now celebrated this valuable book. I'm so very grateful to each one of you.

In many ways, I have written this book for my four sons and their wives, and especially for my grandchildren. I have long thought, "There needs to be a book that would help emerging leaders know the path that lies ahead and within—a sort of road map for the journey each leader takes to learn how to lead well and live well." *Inside Job* is that book for each of you. I hope the pages of this book will be well worn in your own hands. I pray that you will read this book throughout the seasons of your lives—giving careful attention to what I have said here. We all need a light for the path that lies outside of us and within us.

I have a passion for hiking the great outdoors. Those trails seem somehow able to help me come alive. Beldon Lane, author of *The Solace of Fierce Landscapes*, has said, "The wildest, most dangerous trails are always the ones within." But what is true is this: the trail within the heart of everyone who aspires to lead is the most important trail one can ever trek. If you neglect this trail, you will not see what you simply have to see to live well, lead well and be well.

I could not have walked my own trail were it not for my companion in life, Gwen Harding Smith. I have never met a more able travel companion, and it has been my greatest privilege in life to be your companion into your fierce, beautiful and stunning heart. There, I have found glory. There, I have found God.

All blessings, reader, as you begin the trail within to do your Inside Job.

Stephen W. Smith
Potter's Inn at Aspen Ridge
Divide, Colorado

Notes

Chapter 1: Life Is More Than Chasing Success

[1]J. B. Phillips, *The Price of Success* (Wheaton, IL: Harold Shaw Publishers, 1984), p. 9.

[2]Eugene Peterson, "Introduction to 1 and 2 Peter," in *The Message* (Colorado Springs, CO: NavPress, 2006), p. 574.

[3]Thomas Merton, *Love and Living*, ed. Naomi Burton Stone and Brother Patrick Hart (San Diego: Harvest, 1965), p. 11.

[4]Mary Oliver, "Where Are You?," in *Red Bird* (Boston: Beacon Press, 2008), p. 73.

Chapter 2: Signs of the Times

[1]Karl Rahner, *The Need and the Blessing of Prayer*, trans. Bruce W. Gillette (Collegeville, MN: Liturgical Press, 1997), p. 93.

[2]In Europe and elsewhere around the globe, the bells of churches would ring at set hours and times to call people to stop what they were doing and to pray. The French artist Millet painted this scene beautifully in *The Angelus*.

Chapter 3: Comparing the Inner and Outer Markers of Success

[1]Gary L. McIntosh and Samuel D. Rima, *Overcoming the Dark Side of Leadership: How to Become an Effective Leader by Confronting Potential Failures*, rev. ed. (Grand Rapids: Baker Books, 2007).

Chapter 4: Mapping the Journey

[1]Among the leading voices who have helped us are Jean Piaget with his theory of cognitive development, Erik Erikson's stages of psychosocial development and Lawrence Kohlberg's stages of moral development.

[2]Two resources among sociologists and scholars who study faith issues are James Fowler's *Stages of Faith* (New York: HarperOne, 1995) and Janet Hagberg and Robert Guelich's *The Critical Journey*, 2nd ed. (Salem, WI: Sheffield Publishing, 2004).

[3]Mary Oliver, "The Summer Day," in *House of Light* (Boston: Beacon Press, 1992), p. 60.

[4]Hagberg and Guelich, *Critical Journey*.

[5]The word *kenosis* occurs five times in the New Testament: Rom 4:14; 1 Cor 1:17; 9:15; 2 Cor 9:3; and Phil 2:7. In each case the biblical author describes the emptying of Jesus' own self for the sake of others.

[6]I have prepared a chart showing the stages of leadership development along with other pertinent information in the workbook. I believe you'll find this chart beneficial as you find yourself on the leadership journey.

[7]Pierre Teilhard de Chardin, SJ, "Patient Trust," in *Hearts on Fire: Praying with Jesuits* (Chicago: Loyola Press, 2005), pp. 102-3.

Chapter 5: The Great Eight Virtues, Part One

[1]Max De Pree, *Leadership Is an Art* (New York: Dell Publishing, 1989), p. 11.

[2]C. S. Lewis, *Mere Christianity* (New York: HarperCollins, 2001), p. 93.

[3]The spiritual disciplines of silence and solitude are vital to leadership. Just as we are told that "Jesus often withdrew to lonely places and prayed" (Lk 5:16 NIV), we know that leaders must do the same to be grounded and effective. See Ruth Haley Barton's *Invitation to Solitude and Silence* (Downers Grove, IL: IVP Books, 2010) as a primer. Henri Nouwen's *The Way of the Heart* (New York: Ballantine, 1981) should be required reading for every leader who wants to understand the essential, transformative powers of being quiet and alone—alone with God.

[4]Quoted in Kyle Strobel, *Formed for the Glory of God: Learning from the Spiritual Practices of Jonathan Edwards* (Downers Grove, IL: InterVarsity Press, 2013), p. 94.

[5]See the accompanying workbook for resources on ways to know yourself and your dark side.

[6]Brené Brown, *Daring Greatly: How the Courage to Be Vulnerable Transforms the Way We Live, Love, Parent and Lead* (New York: Gotham, 2012), p. 25.

[7]Henri Nouwen, *Out of Solitude: Three Meditations on the Christian Life* (Notre Dame, IN: Ave Maria Press, 2004), p. 38.

[8]I explore this in my book *The Lazarus Life* (Colorado Springs, CO: David C. Cook, 2008).

Chapter 6: The Great Eight Virtues, Part Two

[1]Nelson Mandela, *Long Walk to Freedom: The Autobiography of Nelson Mandela* (London: Abacus Books, 1999), p. 751.

[2]Many Bible commentators connect this verse, "[Jesus] steadfastly set his

face to go to Jerusalem" (Luke 9:51 KJV), with Isaiah 50:7: "Therefore have I set my face like flint, and I know I will not be put to shame" (NIV).

[3]C. S. Lewis, *The Weight of Glory* (New York: HarperCollins, 1980), p. 61.

[4]Eugene Peterson, *A Long Obedience in the Same Direction* (Downers Grove, IL: InterVarsity Press, 1980).

[5]Frederick Buechner, *Secrets in the Dark: A Life in Sermons* (New York: HarperCollins, 2007), p. 144.

[6]Thomas Merton, *New Seeds of Contemplation* (New York: New Directions Publishing, 1972), p. 45.

[7]Dale and Juanita Ryan, NACR Daily Meditation, October 29, 2013, http://two.pairlist.net/pipermail/nacrmed/2013-October/004028.html.

[8]C. S. Lewis, *The Four Loves* (Orlando, FL: Harcourt, 1988), p. 121.

[9]Henri Nouwen, *Life of the Beloved* (New York: Crossroads Publishing, 2012), p. 67.

Chapter 7: The Leader's Rhythm

[1]Thomas Merton, *Conjectures of a Guilty Bystander* (Garden City, NJ: Doubleday, 1966), p. 73.

[2]Wayne Muller, *Sabbath: Finding Rest, Renewal and Delight in Our Daily Lives* (New York: Bantam, 1999), p. 5.

[3]In my book *Soul Custody* (Colorado Springs, CO: David C. Cook, 2010), I develop the concept of Sabbath more fully, and in the workbook you'll find studies and suggestions to consider as you begin ceasing work and enjoying a day God wanted you to enjoy.

[4]Katie Johnson, "For majority of workers, vacation days go unused," *The Boston Globe*, December 30, 2013, www.bostonglobe.com/business/2013/12/30/for-majority-workers-vacation-days-unused/7X1VwsRbVahLOzy98wnTyH/story.html.

Chapter 8: The Leader's Limits

[1]"NFL Hopeful FAQs," NFL Players Association, www.nflplayers.com/About-us/FAQs/NFL-Hopeful-FAQs.

[2]This is a reference that offers God's perspective about regaining the lost years of our lives due to certain "locusts" demolishing our families, health, relationships and more.

[3]Paul Johnson, *Churchill* (New York: Viking Adult, 2009), p. 5.

[4]Ibid.

[5]Copyright 1999-2009 Texas Medical Association. All rights reserved.

[6]John Eldridge, *Desire: The Journey We Must Take to Find the Life God Offers* (Nashville: Thomas Nelson, 2000), p. 8.

[7]Before Paul's conversion we learn that he was a leader in the persecution of men, women and children who followed Jesus. His unredeemed passion resulted in the unfortunate death of many.

Chapter 9: The Leader's Transitions

[1]William Bridges, *Transitions* (Cambridge, MA: Da Capo Press, 2004), p. 3.

[2]Ibid.

[3]Charles Dickens, *Tale of Two Cities* (London: Chapman and Hall, 1859), p. B.

[4]Terry Walling, *Stuck!* (St. Charles, IL: ChurchSmart Resources, 2008), p. xii.

[5]Richard Rohr, *Falling Upward: A Spirituality for the Two Halves of Life* (San Francisco: Jossey-Bass, 2011), pp. 43-44.

[6]Jim Branch, *Room to Flourish: Daily Space with God* (blog), September 19, 2012, http://jb-coreleadership.blogspot.com/2012/09/between-day-3.html.

[7]Bridges, *Transitions.*

[8]Ibid.

[9]John O'Donohue, "A Blessing for One Who Is Exhausted," Awakin.org, July 26, 2011, www.awakin.org/read/view.php?tid=698.

Chapter 10: Living and Leading a Resilient Life

[1]Pierre Teilhard de Chardin, *The Phenomenon of Man* (New York: Harper Perennial, 2008), p. 211.

[2]This is the subtitle for Peter Scazzero's highly recommended book *Emotionally Healthy Spirituality* (Grand Rapids: Zondervan, 2006).

[3]Daniel Duane, "Do Men Suck at Friendship?" *Men's Journal,* May 2014, www.mensjournal.com/magazine/do-men-suck-at-friendship-20140422.

[4]In my other books, I have given attention more in depth to this important human need. Please refer to *Transformation of a Man's Heart* (Downers Grove, IL: InterVarsity Press, 2006); *Soul Custody* (Colorado Springs, CO: David C. Cook, 2010); *The Lazarus Life* (Colorado Springs, CO: David C. Cook, 2008); and *The Jesus Life* (Colorado Springs, CO: David C. Cook, 2012).

[5]I've written a chapter on this subject, "Soul Vocation: Choosing What to Do with Your Life," in *Soul Custody.*

[6]The two most influential books I've read and used with countless others to help with soul and role confusion are Parker Palmer's *Let Your Life Speak* (San Francisco: Jossey-Bass, 2000) and David Whyte's *Crossing the Unknown Sea: Vocation as Pilgrimage to Identity* (New York: Riverhead Books, 2001).

[7]David Whyte, "Rest," in *Consolations: The Solace, Nourishment and Underlying Meaning of Everyday Words* (Langley, WA: Many Rivers Press, forthcoming).

[8]Virginia Postrel, *The Future and Its Enemies: The Growing Conflict over Creativity, Enterprise, and Progress* (New York: Touchstone, 1998), p. 188.

[9]Stuart Brown, "Why Play Is Vital—No Matter Your Age: Stuart Brown on TED.com," TEDBlog, March 12, 2009, http://blog.ted.com/2009/03/12/stuart_brown_play.

Chapter 11: Leading with Contentment and Satisfaction

[1]The many resources that can help you here are listed in the accompanying workbook.

[2]You can read Jesus' teachings in the four Gospels: Matthew, Mark, Luke and John. These passages contain Jesus' insights on contentment: Why we worry over things (Mt 6:25), why we are so concerned about money (Mt 6:19-21), and what really matters in life (Mt 13:44-46).

[3]Anthony De Mello, *The Way to Love* (New York: Doubleday, 1992), p. 4.

For a companion workbook, resources and platform
for discussion, please go to myinsidejob.org.

Potter's Inn

Care of the Soul for the Sake of Others

Potter's Inn is a Christian ministry devoted to the care of the souls of leaders in the marketplace and ministry, so that leaders can in turn care for the souls of those in their spheres of influence. Founded in 2000 by Stephen W. and Gwen Harding Smith, Potter's Inn has five goals:

1. To lead guided retreats for organizations, businesses and churches on the themes of transformation and soul care.

2. To provide soul care for individual leaders through spiritual direction, mentoring and the Soul Care Intensive, a private retreat with a leader/spouse and a staff member of Potter's Inn.

3. To develop resources such as books, small group guides and art. The resources of Potter's Inn have been translated in multiple languages throughout the world and are available at pottersinn.com as well as through local bookstores.

4. To operate our own intimate retreat, Potter's Inn at Aspen Ridge in Divide, Colorado. On thrity-five pristine acres, secluded and surrounded by three mountain ranges, our retreat is available for vacations, retreats and family reunions.

5. To launch the Soul Care Institute, a two to three year training program for leaders in ministry and the marketplace, equipping them to personally embrace the life-changing theme of soul care.

For more information on Potter's Inn, visit pottersinn.com.

To download the Study Guide to *Inside Job* and join the discussion, visit myinsidejob.org.